BOOGIE BOARD MAN

Eight Sessions with Thomas Hugh Morey

by: Mike Del Ninno

1st Edition

Dedicated to Nick and Connie
my loving parents.

Published by Mike Del Ninno
Ormond Beach, Florida USA

Cover photo credit Marilyn Del Ninno

ISBN   979-8-9926241-1-3

Library of Congress Control Number: 2025902861

TABLE OF CONTENTS

"Every board rides a different wave,
and every wave tells a different story."
-Mike Del Ninno

SESSION ONE - THE GATEKEEPER

Out of the five elements of nature (earth, water, fire, air, and space), I've always been drawn to water the most. Something about water takes me to another state of mind, whether it be in the shower or pool, or drizzling rain, and especially when I'm hanging on my bodyboard waiting for another wave set to roll in.

And maybe that's the connection.

I'm still not sure how my initial thoughts surrounding the development of this project surfaced. I think my love of bodyboarding, writing, acting, and film work finally fused into a cohesive project idea, and once that happened, my mind began to race. I jumped online and began researching the boogie board and Tom Morey and pieced together what information I could find.

I wanted more.

Eventually, I stumbled upon a podcast of Tom and Manny Vargas discussing an obscure and abstract subject relating to universal numbers and ancient history. I can't recall the exact content, but it was the strangest conversation. Manny has a long history with the sport of bodyboarding, and he pilots surf trips through his company, EPIC Surf Tours. He also hosts his podcast, BoogLIFE, where he interviews bodyboarders and surf dudes. I decided to track down Manny and send him an email detailing my project idea and requesting contact information for Tom. Shortly after, Manny called and gave me the green light. I can honestly say, without Manny Vargas, none of this project would have moved forward, or at least, not as smoothly.

I was kind of nervous making that call, especially not knowing what to expect. My heart was beating and the anxiety level rising as the phone rang. Then, a female voice answered, *"hello."* I responded tentatively, introduced myself, and asked if Tom Morey was available. *"No, but I'm his wife, Marchia Morey."* During the next ten or so minutes we got to know each other. I mentioned I was from the Daytona Beach area, which springboarded her into a background story of surfing the whole east coast with a friend during the heydays of her youth, including Daytona Beach. So far, no mention of Tom.

I finally realized I was being screened by the protective gatekeeper. I can only imagine how many kooks have called Tom Morey to get his story, or pitch an idea, or simply talk to the creator of the Morey Boogie board. I patiently listened until Marchia simply said, *"here is Tom now,"* and handed off the phone. I guess I passed the test.

BOOGIE BOARD MAN

The first few minutes speaking with Tom I gave him my two-sentence pitch idea of writing a screenplay of his life, expecting the next subject to focus on our relationship. But in typical Tom fashion, he jumped right in and began talking about the legacy of his dad. I got permission to record, and we were on our way. It was like a catharsis had begun. The beginning of a lifelong purge and I was the vessel. We both could tell early on our relationship was going to be truly meaningful. From my end, a subject I had a passion for, and from Tom's, he finally found someone who really cared about digging deep into his life. Our flow was effortless, as I didn't have to quiz him too hard before he would simply begin storytelling. I just had to make sure I kept him on task.

The only uncomfortable discussion we had (at least on my end) revolved around revealing his true inner self. I made it clear I was looking for something real in Tom's life, the ugly with the good. Up until this point, Tom had only dealt with individuals looking for the boogie board story, and maybe his early days with surfing. I wanted the whole package, the warts and all, including life events that weren't already told. I could tell he struggled somewhat, but deep down inside he was dying to let it all out. Once he came to terms, it became real. He didn't seem worried about what people would think, and looking back, I think he knew his days were numbered; he wanted his inner life struggles revealed, alongside the good.

SESSION TWO - THE TERM BOARD

The year was 1935, a time of several monumental events. Amelia Earhart became the first person to successfully fly solo from Honolulu to Oakland, Krueger's Cream Ale sold the first canned beer in Richmond, Virginia, President Franklin D. Roosevelt signed the Social Security Act into law, and Howard Hughes set a new airspeed record of 354.4 mph in his Hughes H-1 Racer plane.

And unbeknownst to the world, Thomas Hugh Morey, born, August 15, 1935, in Detroit, MI. would gift the world with a creation just as monumental, albeit thirty-seven years later.

Born into a hardworking, middle-class family, Tom's dad clearly had an impact on his life's journey. His father left the motor city and headed for New York where he worked at Coney Island operating rollercoasters. His talents expanded to dancing, Sears merchandise manager, and vacuum sales, to name a few. During WWII, he decided to go west, initially Clear Lake, but finally settled in Merced, CA where he bought a combination auto court, trailer park, gas station and general store on Highway 99, for fifteen thousand dollars, which he saved selling vacuum cleaners and sewing machines. Not bad for someone with only a fifth-grade education.

It was here where Tom experienced his musical epiphany, at seven years old. A few classmates were putting on a play and they needed a drummer. He found a garbage can, carved a few wood sticks, and started banging away. The sensation was immediate and life changing, as the chills and goosebumps led to his love of rhythm, a theme that would play out over Tom's musical and surfing career.

After selling the RV park and store for a decent profit, the family traveled to San Diego looking for manufacturing work within the aircraft industry. While stopped in Laguna, Tom's mom was shoe shopping, and the family stumbled into a nearby real estate office. They fell in love with a cute starter home located on 10th Street and bought it for thirty-five hundred dollars. The family settled down and established Morey Real Estate, where Tom discovered his love of water and surf techniques on a surf mat. Tom would strap himself to his father's back while learning how to body surf, usually ending in competitive water fights. Tom also learned the ways of cold water, his dad showing him how to slowly adjust his body temperature by edging into the surf, toes first, then knees, then waist, until finally it felt good to jump in. It was a paramount lesson since the wetsuit hadn't yet been invented.

Music lessons at ten quickly revealed a prodigy percussionist, and by thirteen he was nearly professional, twirling his custom made black and white striped sticks made by his father, his signature move. At fifteen he joined the original Sons of the Beach ukulele band, and his early marketing skills began to emerge as he added hula dancers to the act, entertaining local service members at Kiwanis clubs. One day he was hanging out at Oak Street beach in Laguna bodysurfing with his duck foot swim fins and saw someone heading for the waves with a finless surfboard. He asked if he could borrow it to surf a few waves, and he became hooked with the thrill of motion and rhythm.

While attending Laguna High School, Tom formed his first band Four Eyed Five, outfitted with sunglasses and blue suede shoes. Bandmates included Tom Santley (bass), Larry Brixey (piano), Donnie Hawkins (tenor sax), Tony Mason (tenor sax), with Tom on drums, and his college band, the Tom Morey Quartet, won the 1956 college jazz band competition. Tom, being the audacious promoter, would call local clubs and fraternities for twenty-five-dollar gigs before heading down to experience Los Angeles jazz clubs. In the early 1950s, Dizzy Gillespie would bring the hottest jazz musicians from New York to Los Angeles to capitalize on Hollywood studio work. While in L.A., the greats would head over to The Lighthouse, a famous local spot where club owner, John Levine, started an experimental Sunday jazz session running from 2:00pm to 2:00am. Tom would hang out with Bud Shank, Frank Rosolino, Stan Levey, and

Conti Condoli before being invited on stage to sit in and play with the greats, a tribute to his drumming skills.

Tom's original longing was to join the Navy as a fighter pilot, but due to red-green colorblindness he got washed out of the California ROTC. He found a way to combine his musical talent and patriotism by joining the California National Guard band, playing for dignitaries such as Presidents Nixon and Kennedy, even playing background music to Allen Ginsburg's poetry readings. The persistent persuasion of his father to serve his country led him to sign up for six months of infantry training, where he received the Expert Infantry Badge. The qualifications were sharp shooting, bayonet fighting, camouflage, map reading, leadership skills and as Tom put it, *"You just have to be a highly qualified expert killer, man."*

Tom established his lifesaving skills at the Balboa Bay Club, also known as Hollywood's Riviera, and the Laguna Guard Force. His final odd job was a Disneyland ride operator for Snow White and the Seven Dwarfs, until the boredom led him to quit, and the surfing and music began to call. He became the first person to let go of a towline and surf an ocean wake, although being first is debatable. A few college buddies were out on a friend's forty-five-foot Chris Craft, he jumped in, had the strength to pull up on the rope, dropped into the wave pocket, dropped the rope, and became one of the first wakeboarders on a surfboard.

In 1953 Morey entered the University of Southern California wanting to major in music. He switched to mathematics after realizing music might not pay the bills. Surfing by day, and playing music at night, Tom became one of the hottest longboarders in Laguna.

"I was hot, I was friggin hot, man. My last year in high school and into my freshmen year of college, I was one of those guys when I showed up at the beach, I'd hear them whispering, that's Tom Morey."

He claims the interest was modest because, at this point, there were no surf contests, just word of mouth, or ramblings on school grounds and beach breaks. Tom honed his surfing skills riding for the legacy board makers while concentrating on engineering improvements to surfboards. Tom felt early surfboards were simply not designed correctly, and on this subject, he was straightforward in his opinion. He felt surfers were ignorant, in terms of shaping boards, and really didn't apply engineering principles. His opinion was open to interpretation by the rest of the surfing community but felt most guys simply shaped out of their garage, while he studied engineering and aerodynamics, applying those techniques to increase speed and reduce drag. By 1955 Morey had already invented concave nose pockets and turned down noses for surfboards. He was a sponsored rider for Dave Goodart, Dave Sweet, Velzy-Jacobs and finally Dewey Weber, with each of their boards being disappointments. They were all great board builders, but none provided either the feel or performance Tom sensed was possible.

"We have the term the board, which is demeaning to that watercraft, by calling it a board, which everybody does. But it is a combination of curvatures, densities, flexibilities, and lengths that needs to be designed to fit into the wave under various circumstances and can be repelled by the wave under other circumstances, and to be maneuverable so that you can side slip it, or you can hold it in and then get it out and all these different things that are required of that board. So naturally, for a guy that's gonna be a board builder, none of these boards of these other guys really gave the proper feeling. They were slow here and too fast, well none of them were too fast, but made by guys that had taken woodshop and learned how to work with their hands, but none had been skilled observers of hydrodynamics. And nobody knew how to surf. Nobody on the planet really knew how to surf compared to how they know how to surf now. But compared to how it had been in Hawaii thousands of years earlier or modern Hawaii a hundred years ago or modern California a few years ago, the boards had gotten pretty good, but they were still arcane."

Tom became a sought-after team surfer and one of the early sponsored professionals, always creating original longboard maneuvers. He was known for the standing island pullout, where a surfer stands at the nose and spins the board around until the tail block faces the beach. By the end of high school, he was surfing Trestles, Cotton's, Salt Creek, Malibu and Rincon, all spots reserved for the highly skilled surfer.

Although he had an affinity for engineering, he struggled with formal education. After graduating from high school, he attended USC where night humanities class bored him so badly that he would wake up in a puddle of drool. According to Tom, there is math, and then there is arithmetic, with arithmetic being the primary vehicle for teachers to engage students. However, mathematics is clever stuff. With math you're either right or wrong, and Tom struggled with the subjectivity of professors and the influence they instilled over students. He enjoyed debating and challenging math theories with other students and professors, but thought his English teachers were just a cliché with plaid sweaters, leather elbows, and pipes. His formal education wouldn't yield much, but promised his dad he'd learn how to study and knuckle down, especially since dad was footing the bill. The early years yielded mediocre grades, but by graduation he excelled with A's and B's while becoming adept with his engineering creativity.

Southern California was a hot bed for surfing, shaping, and culture. Everyone was jumping on the surf craze, from garage shapers to Hollywood producers, and the competitive urgency for market dominance drove a mess of untested innovation. Tom had no shortage of crazy ideas. His first failed idea was driven by his competitive desire to beat Hobie Alter, who was transitioning from balsawood to a polyurethane foam surfboard and interchangeable fin system. Most folks probably know Hobie Alter's name from his famous Hobie Cat catamaran.

"Hobie had a natural knack for business and tooling, as well as a personality that really connected with folks, and he was my archrival through life."

The rivalry apparently began in high school, as Hobie and Tom dated the same girl, Sharon. Oddly enough, they also both dated another Sharon during college. Tom and Sharon separated, but Hobie nonetheless asked Tom for permission to date. Tom gave his permission and Hobie and Sharon eventually married.

"He was a true gentleman, a barefoot gentleman."

In his quest to locate the polyurethane foam for his version of a foam surfboard, Tom called Douglas Aircraft, where an engineer suggested he not use polyurethane foam, but rather a safer alternative material, Douglas Aircomb, an expandable paper honeycomb soaked with resin. On a whim, Tom requested a sample and received a 50-pound package. With his friend and classmate, Bob Tierney, they attempted to build out a surfboard, but the integrity of the board failed miserably in the water.

"Well, paper honeycomb comes only so wide, so we cut two- or three-inch-thick pieces that were in regular width and figured out how to glue them together using contact cement and make a thing that approximated a surfboard shape, a blank. And then from that, band sawed it out with a better plane shape, and then using a disc sander, sanded it into a better shape, and then fiberglassed it. Now fiberglassing is very hard because it's all just edges, so you need

something to set it on that will accept a variety of shape contours. So I got a big plastic bag and put a separate sheet of polyethylene on top of the bag, and then a resin-soaked fiberglass piece, and then set the honeycomb on that expanded to a decent approximation of the shape with some weight on that, not too much weight, and suspended that on top of the plastic bag. So, anyhow, the catalyst went off, and it got hot, which I hadn't calculated in. It got so hot that it burned through the bag and dropped out to the cement floor. So we made the best of that, patched that up with some fiberglass and did it on the other side, and made this horrible thing. But it was kind of a surfboard and got it down to the water one Friday night to Saint Ann's Street, and Joey Cabell was out there, who was a very hot Hawaiian surfer before he opened the Chart House restaurants, and I said let me try your board because he had a Velzy Pig, a different shape board. So we traded boards, and he caught one wave on this thing, and he lost it, and walking in to retrieve it, finally picked the board up, but both ends stayed in the water because it had broken in half."

Not knowing what to do with the left-over material, they headed over to USC's architectural lab and began to experiment with building various paper novelties, and on the advice of a friend, settled on a honeycomb paper hat. He made three dozen, took them to a bar, and sold eleven for three dollars each. The hat creation was featured on the cover of Parade Magazine leading to tens of thousands of Fan Topper Hats selling in L.A. novelty stores. His first attempt at a foam surfboard failed, but his first novelty venture was a tremendous financial success, provoking a rebellious streak with Tom wanting more.

It was at USC where he met his first wife, Carolyn (Jolly) Givens. Jolly was a Delta Gamma and member of Kappa Pi, a national Honorary art fraternity at USC from which she graduated cum laude. Tom was a Phi Delta Theta and noticed Jolly during rush week.

"I met her at Presents, where she was one of the cuter girls at the sorority house, and I remembered her a little bit from that. But somehow she remembered me, and one day I'm walking down the aisle in the auditorium at USC, and she walked up to me and smiled, I smiled back, and that's the only girl that had stopped and smiled at me. I got word from a friend, who was a hasher, she was attracted to me and would like to go out with me."

They were married at St Edmund's Episcopal Church, San Marino, CA on Jolly's parents thirtieth wedding anniversary, December 20, 1958, in front of three-hundred-and-fifty guests. They had two daughters and divorced after twelve years. It was hard to assess the true relationship between Tom and Jolly, as he was somewhat vague in communicating what drove them apart.

"After the whole thing (divorce), she credits me as one of the main things of her life, and that I turned her on to the ocean, and I turned her on to science. She told me, 'Tommy, she says, before I knew you, I didn't know that people thought, I didn't understand what thinking was,' and I could tell that from her letters. They were not thoughtful; they were so purposeless. I could never get into conversations with her. Then after we were married, she took her first science class, and she

really took to biology and chemistry, and she was smitten by science and thinking. And we're pretty good friends to this day."

Can you sum up why you split?

"It's just not quite right. She summed it up this way, she said, 'Tommy, she said, our marriage was like, your family has a dog on a leash and my family has a dog on a leash, and finally, instead of each family holding on to the far end of the leash, they tied the far ends together and off go the two dogs running down the road.' And as for the attraction part of her, to me, is that she's art....she's this....I don't know what the hell, I'm trying to put it into words, fuck words."

Whatever reason for the attraction, then split, it wasn't before Jolly had an atypical impact on Tom's life leading to his boogie destiny, as colorful events leading up to their divorce were about to unfold.

Our conversation was approaching an hour, and we both needed a break. As we closed out our second session, I asked Tom whether he wanted to include any family members to expand on our story. I was aiming to get some collaboration and different points of view. Although he made his love of family clear, I perceived a guardedness, and possible caution, on what family storylines may be introduced. Maybe some family members didn't want to participate in the project. Whatever the reason, Tom made it clear he wanted to control the narrative. It was Tom's story, as told by the man himself.

SESSION THREE - A ZILLION DINGS

During the first two conversations it was easy to keep Tom on task. We were still feeling each other out, in terms of whether we trusted each other enough to really commit to a life story, let alone write a screenplay. Tom's main concern was my lack of experience within the entertainment industry, which was well founded since my writing experience was limited to blogs, short films, and a stage play. In my opinion, my love of bodyboarding and deep passion for the project easily made up for any inexperience. As the magnitude of the project began to sink in, worries surfaced concerning my ability to sift through and organize mounds of data related to his life. So, during those first two sessions we were both careful not to plunge ourselves into uncomfortable life subjects. I began with simple questions concerning his early days, leading to USC. His responses were concise and straightforward.

However, what happened at the start of our third session was a delightful surprise.

I realized we had the makings of an entertaining story, worthy of producing, either into a screenplay, or a book.

Tom must have felt the same way; by letting me know how impressed he was with my initial research on his life uncovering things no one had ever inquired about. I explained how moviegoers or readers must feel his pain, sorrow, and failures, in addition to his joy, or we'd just be revealing the same old "making of the boogie board." Tom agreed. The walls came down, and Tom and I got real, as he began to share his thoughts about telling his life story.

"OK, my thoughts on it are there's an overall wave that's been breaking. I drew a picture of a guy surfing a wave, and he's like going towards the barrel and he's thinking about how he's riding that wave. But as you zoom back, you see that it's just a little teeny piece of chop on a huge wave that is already breaking, because everything is in free fall. Nobody's aware of it, and that's what's going on right now. The entire makeup of the planet, our whole paradigm, or whatever the stations are, are just collapsing. The whole wave is changing. So there's this major action taking place, and the guys that are jazz musicians and experimenters and inventors are a little further along in seeing what's going on. And so I'm quite a long way on perceiving the downfall and at the same time the growth that springs up. It's kind of like a bazooka with stuff going out the front but also going out the back. Stuff going up, and then there's stuff going down. So my main interest is in showing those who read this how to surf life, and in these circumstances, how to hold on in the barrel and all that kind of stuff."

I simply replied, *"do you think we can accomplish that by sharing your difficulties and obstacles, and how you've overcome them throughout your life?"*

He replied humbly, *"Yes, I think we can do that."*

We went from a biographical timeline to heavy philosophy. In that moment, I saw a totally different side of Tom, one that was rooted in deep thought, philosophy, religion, and celestial belief. I didn't have to ask him to expand on the metaphor, I totally got it, and Tom knew I got it. Trust and friendship were formed, as we recognized our time spent together would be something special, even if only for us. It became obvious, the authentic Tom Morey had an unusual way of communicating his thoughts, as his brain processed differently than most, with futurist, visionary, inventor, musician, surfer, shaper, engineer, wheeler dealer, and philosopher all simultaneously competing for grey matter. I accepted the challenge of interpreting his metaphoric viewpoints. Tom's beliefs were beginning to reveal himself, as he felt our universe was breaking and constantly changing, both for the better and worse. On a celestial level, we're only an ant colony, not noticing what's happening around us. And inventive and artistic individuals are at the forefront of understanding. He believed small ambiguous life events, rather than the obvious, shaped him as a man.

"So there are little side events that happen, maybe you bump into a guy, or you sit next to him that can still turn out to be influential. When my parents owned the trailer park in Merced, it was next to Anderson's motel, and a family moved in there for a few days, and I got to know this kid and we played together. And my God, whereas I was running around and playing simple minded stuff, this kid played

and was building an aircraft carrier with the various decks, and inside on each level, teeny airplanes were aligned certain ways. This kid was an incredible genius builder, and he taught me in just a few play sessions, how much more can be bitten and how much more can be done in detail. So, playing with this kid for a couple of afternoons led to monumental change."

Whatever it was that ran the show here on the planet, it was all a plan leading to his boogie destiny. He wasn't just a one trick pony, or some guy that got lucky once. He embraced the boogie fame but wanted to be accepted for so much more. The love of creation and invention drove his circle of friends, and internal conflict became a common theme throughout his life. Tom gravitated to the changes and chances of the universe, especially those producing goose bumps, chills, and thrills.

"I'm taken by people that say and do interesting things, and it's not the love of some particular ant in the ant colony, it's about there actually being an ant colony and there being a higher order. And we have a problem where, as soon as this goes to a certain level, it becomes God and God's manifestation for this day and age, and Jesus and Buddha, all that kind of stuff. And it goes sideways into churchianity. And fuck that shit, man. There is God and God's creation, and God is undefinable, greater than every great one and undefinable, and we're part of it and we're little, teeny trolls, little, teeny buglets inside an enormous entity. We are part of an enormous being, and that's what escapes the writer and the reader and the teller. A listener watches and hears something from somebody and then worships a pair of lips,

instead of recognizing the person that's saying the thing, or worships some God or guy or gal, instead of getting with the bigger program."

Fame was not something Tom was chasing, nor did he embrace the fame of others. He was drawn to a circle of friends that wanted to have an influence on the planet. And in the early sixties, in Malibu, that circle of friends usually revolved around the arts and surfing. It was clear Tom believed he was part of a higher calling, a small bit of humanity within an infinite galactic universe. He was conflicted with religion, in that churchianity wasn't the answer. But, at what point in his life did he come to that realization, and why? Although I loved the spontaneous interview style, if I ever wanted to find out, I needed to get back on task. I quickly pivoted back to surfing and his early days at USC, asking him, *"how did you get so good at surfing?."* I was anticipating a detailed response outlining his practice regimen, and ways he learned to nose ride and work the board, but was surprised with his simple answer.

"I had a car, that's how I became good. And, I had nothing else better to do, because there isn't anything else better to do than to go surfing. Play music or go surfing, you know, and when you come out of the water, there's nothing better to do than to go plop down in the sand, soaking wet and pull that hot sand up around underneath your chest and your shoulders and hunker down out of the breeze, out of the wind, and lay there and absorb the sun like a lizard. And after you get too hot, there's nothing better in the world to do than to run into the water

and do it again. And once you get started on surfing and music, well then, there it is, you've got sex, you've got love…"

Tom had a natural knack for the moves of the day. He downplayed the romantic side of surfing and zeroed in on the daily mundane tasks required to get to the beach, paddle out and catch waves. I dug deeper searching for some dreamy storyline, *"did you ever get injured, or encounter sharks or have a major wipeout?."*

"All the time, but it's not injured like some author can turn into a big deal. Let me tell you about injuries. I came out of eight inches of water and I just kind of moved my foot for some reason, and I hit a rock, and I broke my foot. Not some big 20-foot wave. It's a zillion little dings, a zillion little getting hit. Everything from being out in the sun too long and suffering sunburn and having my mother making ice, making tea, and putting rags soaked with tea on my sunburned back to try and heal that thing. Years just walking along the beach and you step on somebody's lit cigarette in the sand, and you burn the hell out of your foot. Everything like that, a sliver from the wood on the boardwalk, all the way up to walking out on the rocks and gently bumping against a sea urchin which has little ceramic spines that are rounded on the bleeding edge. I had one that went in near my big toe and it came out a year and a half later. Then you get bumped getting in and out of the car and getting your board off and your board falls, and it breaks, and now you've got to repair the ding. And that leads to standing in fiberglass, and then more slivers are in your body. All kinds of little dingy bumpy things that are going on, and the romance

is maybe in front of the cameraman, but the reality is all this fucking greasy bumping going on."

Our sessions were becoming a haphazard discussion of life stories and philosophies, with no structured sequence, and I wasn't about to interrupt the free flow of memories rushing through Tom's brain. I was simply along for the ride.

SESSION FOUR – NOSERIDING

Each session had a different energy and flow, and this time I could sense that Tom wasn't feeling on top of his game. It wasn't clear if this was due to ongoing health issues, but unless he willingly served up information, I respected Tom's privacy. I decided to ease him back to a biographical timeline, asking how he met his lifelong friend, Bob Tierney. Reminiscing about his days at USC brought his energy level up, and I needed to move the story along to understand his transition from college to surf shop. Tierney (as Tom called him) was a red-haired guy with glasses who sat next to Tom in their freshman math class. Tom moved out of the Phi Delta Theta house during his junior year, and at Bob's invitation, moved in with Tierney and his mother rent-free, where they spent hours discussing surfboard design, especially learning from failed contraptions like the honeycomb surfboard. Tierney was Tom's best man and later would play a pivotal role in making Tom's boogie dream a reality.

The surf crew also included Karl Pope, another friend from USC. Karl began dating one of their classmates, Olympic diver Paula Jean Myers, whom he eventually married. Paula Jean won 11 Nationals, 2 Pan Am titles and a total of 4 Olympic medals. She also won the U.S. Olympic Trials in 1960 and won the silver medal in Rome. This Olympic relationship would later spark an idea for Tom's first innovative noseriding contest. Karl transferred in from Hollywood High School and was a few years behind Tom. His fun personality made him an instant hit. The crew would pool gas money for surf trips, and both had a love of music, namely playing ukulele. This friendship led to Tom's next shared experiment, the Surfboard Suitcase. Karl's original idea was to design a foldable surfboard for easy travel. After a few failed attempts, and tapping into Tom's manufacturing skills, Karl paid Tom to build a few prototypes, which they tested on a surf trip to Mexico while filming an advertisement. Karl eventually registered the patent, but the board never gained commercial viability.

"The thing about that is the surfboard is jointed in two places; it's three pieces and held together like suitcase luggage. The thing is going click, clack, and it's not very stable. It's gonna break apart any minute. It weighs forty-five pounds and I'm very careful not to break it. I'm just going through any kind of BS movements to look like it's really surfable. This was only an advertisement, and I'm not pushing the limits because I'm going to break the board if I do."

Southern California culture continued to evolve and so did Tom's rebellious nature. El Cholo Restaurant was a favorite among USC students and local Hollywood celebrities. The crew would roll in without shoes on all-you-can-eat night and engage in free-thinking discussions. Tom was beginning to diverge from his middle-class upbringing, as non-conformity began to drive his independence. He served his six months of infantry training, but only as a quid pro quo with his father to continue his surfing and band activities. His patriotism and love of country was in direct contradiction to the emerging counterculture of the time, creating his first internal struggle.

"I wasn't involved at all with the nation. I hated the mandatory pledging my allegiance to the United States of America, or to China, or whatever the hell it was......blah, blah, blah, blah, everybody's dancing....blah blah blah blah. Decades later I was over in Taiwan, and I went to a movie, and before the movie the outer curtain went up, and there was this beautiful scene of these Redwood trees and the rain coming through and the light shining from the moon or something, and then they played this Taiwanese music, and it was a pledge of allegiance to the Taiwan nation, or government, or whoever it was. And I realized, Jesus, we're all programmed from day one to pay so much in love with this particular group or political leaders, you know, fuck."

If you took this quote out of context, you might label Tom as not being a patriot, but you'd be wrong. He loved his country and all it had to offer. What he disliked was the "mandatory" part of pledging allegiance to anything, the forcing and brainwashing bestowed on him since his youth. Freedom and choice were at the core of creation, and his conservative childhood began to clash with his liberal adulthood.

Married with two children brought financial responsibilities. He was shaping surfboards out of his garage to keep pace with Hobie and Dave Sweet, but that wasn't paying the bills, plus the plastics and materials necessary to build boards were expensive. That led Tom into the aerospace industry, where he could gain access and learn about advanced materials. Tom landed positions at Avco Corporation and Western Fiberglass before his previous connection researching Douglas Aircomb paid off. In 1959, Morey began work with Douglas Aircraft in Santa Monica as a composite engineer, working with different aspects of composite materials for missile nose cones, rocket nozzles, and filament winding. Tom worked on the high-profile Nike Zeus anti-ballistic missile system, or ABM. The system was designed to destroy incoming Soviet intercontinental ballistic missile warheads before they could hit their targets. Tom's creative drive was only somewhat satisfied at Douglas having the freedom to develop a few minor innovations. But after a few years, he became bored with corporate life.

"Every day I'd see this guy come back from the cafeteria with spilled ketchup on his tie and imagined that would be me for the next ten years."

Tom's internal struggle between a structured corporate life and shaping surfboards out of his garage finally collided. He ditched the job security and salary, borrowing five thousand dollars from his father (a substantial amount back in the 1960's) to open his first surf shop, Morey Skeg Works. He selected Ventura, a town far enough from Manhattan Beach and existing board makers to limit local competition, and close to Rincon, California's premier winter surf spot. During the early months setting up shop, he lived with another influential classmate, Ken Price.

"I met this guy, Kenny Price, who was a character at USC same age as me, actually six months older, right across the Zodiac. He was a grubby guy, his teeth were all green, and his old Ford was a scroungy thing. He was smitten with noseriding and surfboards, whereas that was the big deal in Malibu. But this guy was very funny, and he spoke with an interesting accent…well, we hung out together surfing, and later on before I moved up to Ventura and started the surf shop I just gave him a call, and without asking, he said, 'why don't you come up and stay with me?' He had a great place right on the beach. So I hung out with him for months as I put my shop together in Ventura, and he turned me on when I was a jazz musician, listening to the best guys I could get a hold of, and he had knowledge of all these other players, and he was a pretty good piano player himself, and so he really turned me on to the more progressive jazz, and he turned me on to being a conscientious builder. So he built ceramic pieces that would be like a shape of a potato, and the color of a potato…and not interesting, but with little worm holes in it. And if you look at the worm hole, it was built very carefully with vibrant motorcycle paints with a tiny, tiny brush in there, and these things would sit on pedestals. Well, he became

a world-famous sculptor, and his pieces were on display at LACMA (Los Angeles County Museum of Art) for a two month exhibit there."

After spending a few months with Ken Price, surfing, smoking, and grooving to progressive jazz while drinking tons of coffee as the morning sun rose over the beach, Tom's dream of owning his own surf shop became a reality. Morey Skeg Works opened in 1964, and I speculated, midway through his marriage, whether hanging with Ken Price and leaving the security of Douglas Aircraft may have been the beginning of the end with Jolly. Nonetheless, Tom finally hit it big creating the first polypropylene fin, leading to the first commercially successful interchangeable fin system. This was also the first hint of Tom's creative genius originating witty names and acronyms for his inventions, as his ability to see humor in all things, day in and day out, was a cherished gift that lived within him daily.

"I looked at that thing…this is my mind working at it's very best. So what am I gonna call this thing? I got it. What is this material here? Polypropylene. That's not gonna go anywhere, you know, nobody's gonna remember squat like that, right? So what is it made of? It's made of Polypropylene. What's Polypropylene? Well, it's propane gas, but what is propane gas? Well its plant and animal gas that's been aged for a long time. It's right in there with methane, and propane, and all the other things panes, and it's a gas from the time a dinosaur farts. Now fart spelled backward, TRAF, now that sounds like it's high-tech stuff, TRAF786 or something."

A subsequent product success was Slipcheck, a grit aerosol spray available in colors designed to spray on the nose of the board to assist with traction while riding. At its peak, Slipcheck sold a few hundred thousand units at three and a half dollars per can.

The surf industry was exploding, and Morey Skeg Works quickly outgrew their two tin shacks and fifty-dollar monthly rent, as well as Tom's business acumen to keep pace. His love of creation and inventing equally matched his indifference for managing inventory, cash flow, and balancing capital needs, so he enlisted his USC classmate Karl Pope as an investor and partner. Karl had business skills and social graces that Tom lacked, and bringing Karl onboard freed Tom to focus on promoting the newly formed Morey-Pope Surfboards. Rumor has it, Pope pressed Morey on his name being first but lost. Tom discards the rumor as bullshit. They moved to a larger location, after releasing their rent obligations to Yvon Chouinard, the founder of Patagonia. The Morey-Pope relationship continued to blossom as the two co-founded the Water Apparatus and Vehicular Engineering Corporation, aptly named by Tom as WAVE. The company was created to design various surf and water related inventions, alongside Morey-Pope Surfboards.

His next order of business was to get himself elected as President of the United States Surfing Association, which led to his innovative noseriding contest. Tom was a master of disguising his rebellious nature with good looks, collegiate attire and camera-friendly appearance, which helped him secure the votes necessary to win the election.

"Some guys in Laguna started the first surfing association, the United States Surfing Association. They were successful at beginning it, but not staying with it, because who wants to stay with such a dry thing? And so came an election and this thing had rules for running this contest and I objected to the way the rules were. I didn't like anything about it...I got myself elected as the president...I was the second President of the United States Surfing Association...I had the qualifications and so I nominated myself and got myself elected. And still I couldn't budge this thing, I couldn't get it to go anywhere, and I didn't like my own rules after a while, but I did like the idea of track and field and other activities where it's either yay or nay, but it's not dependent on judgments. It's not dependent on somebody judging if you pointed your toes or not. It has to do with did you clear the pole at fifteen feet two inches or not. Did you jump high over the thing at six feet or not? How far did you put the shot? How fast did you run the hundred-yard dash? All that stuff, and I wanted surfing, and I still want surfing to be that way, and that's why I held this noseriding contest. Ah ha, I'll call the front part of this thing, which everybody does already call it, but I'll call it the nose, too. But I'll give it dimensions. And I picked out of the air, which I have done quite often on a lot of things, including prices to sell stuff, I picked out the first 25% of the board, that is what the nose is. And we'll paint that a special color, and each judge will have assistants that have binoculars and let's say on or off. When the guy gets on the colored part that's the first 25%, or not, we'll compile the time of each judge's observation for

each contestant, and we'll give them plenty of time to ride enough wave so we can really see who can get up on the front part and stay there and nose ride."

Tom was successful in eliminating subjectivity, while brilliantly promoting Slipcheck. The Tom Morey Invitational noseriding contest was a huge success, albeit with no national television coverage, not necessarily a major event. The top twenty-five surfers were invited, and the event was promoted through all the local surf shops, with a fifteen-hundred-dollar prize for the winner(s). Corky Carroll won goofy-foot division, and Mickey Muñoz beat out Mike Hynson, although it was later discovered, due to a scoring error, Mike Hynson was robbed by less than a second. John Severson (founder of Surfer) shot photos for the magazine, and Bruce Brown (Endless Summer) filmed it in color for posterity. Other surfers in the field included David Nuuhiwa, Dewey Weber, Mike Doyle, Skip Frye, Johnny Fain, and Donald Takayama.

Tom's serendipitous boogie journey continued with an unexpected phone call from New York City.

"Out of the blue I got a phone call from my friend Lynn Bailey, a Malibu friend that had broken out of Beverly Hills where he lived with his parents and gone to UCLA and gone to New York City to make his way and got himself a really good job with Kidder Peabody. And he was at a high-end advertising party with the agents from Ogilvy and Mather. This is right out of Mad Men; it's like a Mad Men deal. He's at the party, and they're talking about hiring Dewey Weber. He

overhears that....and asks them, what about Dewey Weber. Turns out International Paper Company is going to make a paper surfboard and ride it in the big waves of Hawaii, and they chose Dewey Weber. But Dewey is too busy and can't do it, so my friend Bailey speaks up and he says, ... 'I got a guy who can do that job, his name is Tom Morey.' And so he gets me the job and they give me a call, and I say, yea, I can make that thing, send me out the materials, let me take a look at it. They send a pallet of partially waterproof paper, and they're making a new cardboard that will withstand water. So I get the materials, and I figure out how to make a surfboard out of it and send them a picture, but the guy says no, I think I'll come up and take a look at it. So they show up from New York, and this is the advertising business, right? How many people show up, about six or seven, maybe eight. Hey, it's a free trip to California in the middle of November."

The gig sent Tom to Makaha on O'ahu where film director, Al Jenkins, was shooting an International Paper commercial launching a new cardboard product designed to hold up on rain-soaked loading docks. The commercial turned out to be a comedy of errors as the initial board broke in two after Tom stuck the wave. Having backup materials, Tom quickly glassed two additional boards the next day and paddled back out into heavy surf. The first board proved useless, but the second board held up long enough for Tom to land the perfect ride. Unfortunately, the camera wasn't rolling, so he headed out on a broken surfboard, patched together a short ride and Jenkins finished the commercial alongside editing magic. The commercial ran during the Apollo 11 moonshot, July 1969, and a photo spread appeared in Life magazine. The payday from the commercial was a substantial, three-thousand dollars for building the first board, one-thousand dollars for each back up board, and approximately five-thousand dollars in television advertising royalties, but more importantly, the experience left him yearning for the island lifestyle.

SESSION FIVE - MORALLY SIDEWAYS

Morey-Pope Surfboards produced a slew of profitable surfboard successes from 1965 towards the end of 1969 including the Snub, Peck Penetrator, Blue Machine, and Camel. Likewise, Slipcheck and TRAF were injecting cashflow to finance expanding inventory, as well as Tom's inventive addiction. He was living the uninhibited lifestyle of the sixties, smoking weed and enjoying cameo roles for various film makers, including Dale Davis and Bruce Brown. These early films were symbolic of the times and were shown at local high school gymnasiums as a way of promoting local talent and selling boards. As we moved the conversation out of the sixties, I detected a swing in mood, as multiple forces of the cosmos would begin to collapse inside Tom's world.

"The surfboard business was changing so radically that almost everybody I knew was going out of business. All the regular surfboard makers which were Velzy, Hobie, Jacobs, Bing, Greg Noll, Dewey Weber, and others...had bought fishing boats and moved up to Northern California and were swordfishing or they just gave up on the whole surfboard business, because the boards were no longer

manufactured by us, but rather you could buy the blanks from Walker foam or Clark foam relatively inexpensively. And you could do all this fiberglass work and shaping yourself in your own garage, and you could sell as cheaply as you wanted, just to get started. So, surfboards went from typically between nine feet six inches long, down to six and a half or seven and a half feet long, with everything topsy turvy because such a short board, although it didn't paddle very well, could get closer to the barrel of the wave and could be shipped easier and more inexpensively."

With a shift away from noseriding, Slipcheck became obsolete, and with surfers seeking the barrel, technological changes were also affecting TRAF, the removable fin system.

"My skegs were injection molded plastics, and they had a certain amount of flexibility, which we were advertising the benefits of, because they were more durable, and they gave a certain snap to your turn because you could bend into your weight and movement and the board would rebound with a spring…surfing changed…and was all about Bonsai pipeline and the big wedge in Hawaii and to ride those waves, the guys didn't want anything that was moving around or tricky at all, they just wanted a stiff, straight, old fashioned fiberglass, skeg. And that was taking its toll…there was just no business for us."

The industry was evolving, and surf manufacturers not anticipating the shift were forced to shut down or re-invent their paradigm of surfing. As much as Tom was a visionary and futurist, he struggled with abandoning the timeless style of surfing longboards, and felt the industry was falling apart.

Financial pressures were intensifying at Morey-Pope Surfboards, as raw materials and unfinished goods dominated the balance sheet, and finished longboard inventory wasn't selling. Not to mention, they had to carry account receivables from customers feeling the same financial pain. The Morey-Pope relationship was straining, and continued development of the Trisect (Surfboard Suitcase) was becoming a drag on capital. No test marketing or research had ever been conducted. They simply built it assuming it would sell, even though it turned out to be expensive, under engineered, and too heavy for surfers to carry around. Oh, and let's not forget the IRS, as Morey would say, *"they're always there, they're always right there, they're ready."*

The anxiety was building and his experimental nature led him to marijuana for a possible solution. I asked Tom, *"when did you start and stop smoking marijuana?,"* knowing it may lead us down a rabbit hole. As someone who smokes weed myself, I found the answer particularly amusing, given our generational gap, and down the hole we went.

"I started when I was in the surfboard business in Ventura, and as a result I started having another whole slant on things, and I started to experiment...I got new insights, and I did some tests. At first I smoked a little marijuana and then I smoked some spinach. My first wife, Jolly, for my birthday, she gave me some dried spinach, dried alfalfa and dried something else. And I found that the spinach joint, if you light it up, it tastes very much like marijuana...so I realized

that all these plants are available for perception when you burn them. And what they're really doing is they're giving up their life, which has been contained in a plant, and they are not giving it away...I don't know how to term it, but you are availed to the spirit and the technology of the plant, the plant gets in you, and you are the plant."

The spinach story caught me off guard, so I asked whether he really caught a buzz from spinach, *"So, are you talking about real spinach like spinach, spinach?"*

Tom replied.

"Well, you got some terms (buzz) that are your own terms that don't correlate with my world at all. Here's what you can do, you can dry some spinach (me laughing), and you can put some of these dried leaves on the electric range, the burner, and waft the smoke...and see what you perceive, and you'll realize it's not so much about marijuana, or some particular thing, but it's a matter of waking up to your perceptions that are coming at you all the time and paying more attention to what your environment is, and also not becoming so easily attached to everything that you're taking in, everything from your hamburger bun to your corn..."

I wasn't sure if he was talking about the munchies, but after a good laugh, we crawled out of the rabbit hole and back to the reality of how marijuana really affected Tom's moral judgement.

The industry shift, financial pressures and failing marriage threw Tom into depression, and he was yearning for a new life in Hawaii.

"I kind of went sideways morally, I started smoking marijuana and turns out I really don't need marijuana to be who I am…it puts me a little over the top and puts me out there and it impedes moral judgment…smoking the marijuana awakened me to the fact that I really was not happy in the marriage I was in, no fault of hers, but it just was the wrong person and holding on to try and make this thing work and all this stuff…"

Tom's getaway plan began while filming the International Paper commercial at Makaha. After the shoot, he swung over to Kaua'i where he fell in love with island life, contacted a real estate agent, and stumbled upon the perfect property, a four-acre house complete with gardens and fruit trees for forty-two thousand five-hundred dollars. He bought it on the spot, cash, no dickering. The payment was accumulated from the commercial shoot, as well as stashed savings, but not before repaying his father's loan.

The second phase involved divesting his fifty percent share of Morey-Pope Surfboards by simply leaving it to Karl and walking away.

The final phase would set the stage for a carefree series of events leading up to the boogie revelation. Although still married, Tom and Jolly were living liberated lives. Jolly had moved on to other relationships, and Tom was cleaning up his life. Not wanting to separate the family, Tom convinced Jolly to move with him to Kaua'i, she reluctantly agreed, but only if she could bring her boyfriend, John Bubinski.

"…I wanted to continue with my family…Jolly, my first wife, had gotten involved with some other guy, and she came over reluctantly, and we sold our place in Ventura, and we came over with Jolly and with her lover, and of course the girls, and the dog Boomerang, and we're all friends, and the lover was a very good friend of mine (laughing), and it was so friendly, it was so nice."

The family packed up their belongings and headed to Kaua'i, only to find out, upon arrival, the shipping vessel with their belongings had been held up in transit. Tom got word of free housing available at an abandoned sugar mill.

"So after we settled in there with John Bubinski, and Jolly and the girls, and we're now living at Kaneshiro's Camp, which is Filipinos worker shacks that have fallen down when the whole sugar cane industry started collapsing, and we lived there because our furnishings didn't come for three months, and it was supposed to be six weeks…and we moved over there and waited, and they never came. So for quite a while, we lived at this camp, which was free housing, and it was a real hippie family deal with Jolly and I and her lover, who is my buddy, and the girls and our dog boomerang…and we're going surfing, and we're going out and picking avocados."

The weight of responsibility was lifted, and spirituality became his new addiction. To compensate for giving up weed, he shifted attention towards Transcendental Meditation, fasting and seriously researching religion. Tom wasn't particularly religious as a youth, and in fact, he began questioning the teachings at the young age of fourteen.

"My mother was an Episcopalian, and my father was nothing and didn't go to church except a couple of times during weddings or something. And in Laguna we lived across the street from a congregation, and we kids went either there, or one of two other places on Sundays. And I went there for a while, and he was a nice minister and did a good job and told the stories about Joshua and Jericho and all that kind of stuff. But at age 14, one day I started going across the street to church, it was a beautiful day in Laguna, and I simply went downtown, which was a block away and went bodysurfing. I'm out there and I'm looking around at the sky, and the clouds, and the planet, and the green, all that kind of stuff that's in the psalms, and I just thought this is the real church, I don't know about that other thing, but this is the real church. And it led to wanting answers to my real questions, then and now, which is, if God is my father, my father's father, well then, who's God's father? And if you keep going on that…what's it go back too? So at age 14, I went into kind of a tailspin, I wanted to know, I wanted to have some foundation to go on, come on, I wanted some answers. So my parents brought in the minister from across the street, and his whole thing was in the Bible it says this, the Bible says that…and I forget what you call logic when you're using the premise as the conclusion…"

Tom's grounding in engineering and math threw some doubt over his religious beliefs, as a premise requires facts to support a logical conclusion, and in this case, the conclusion was being supported by unsubstantiated evidence, which translates into faith. Our commonality regarding this subject was shared, we both believed a higher power existed in the universe, we just couldn't comprehend where, or how it was originated, and by whom. Two things pulled him out of his tailspin.

"One, a friend of mine said, 'Morey, you see that tree over there? That tree is there, I don't know why it's there, you don't know why it's there, nobody knows why it's there, how is it possible? So join the crew and the club and quit pissing and moaning.' The other thing that pulled me out was ice cream, chocolate ice cream is such a solution, it's such a remover of difficulties."

Tom had come full circle on his quest to understand religion by researching several books, The Lost Teachings of Jesus and The Essene Gospel, both having a major influence on his religious viewpoint and way of life.

"They each portrayed Jesus in a slightly different light, different language, the same feeling...Jesus in each of these books was the same guy, the same kind of practical no nonsense, straight ahead thinking...it just started opening me up a great deal ...when a guy removes smoking, drinking, gambling, and chasing women from his life, there's a whole lot of time to do other neat stuff."

The nearby Kaua'i library became an oasis for religious research, while surfing and picking avocados filled the rest of his day. He was slowly transitioning from board thumper to deep thinker, while still nurturing his impetuous reaction to opportunistic situations. Our sessions churned out a lot of laughs, and I anticipated most would come from surf-related stories, but Tom never laughed so hard until he told the Mexican restaurant story, and I could tell from his amusement; the offbeat experience really spoke to his spontaneous nature.

The story began, *"The Mexican restaurant came about as a result of…there was a Mexican restaurant."*

The restaurant was owned by a girl named Gail and was the first Mexican restaurant on the island. Tom and the family would trade avocados and papayas for dinner. One day, Gail is so down, and so upset, she's sick of being in a failing restaurant business, and wants to move over to Honolulu, where her boyfriend lives so they can marry. Tom loves Mexican food, but all he can do is console Gail and keep bringing her avocados, hoping she survives.

Shortly before the family moved to Kaua'i, they drove through Oxnard, spotting a few Burma Shave styled signs for a road-side dive. Burma signs were a series of small, humorous, rhyming signs posted along US highways in the 1920s through the 1960's, and were designed to be read by motorists, each revealing a rhyme until the final sign revealed the product name. Tom was a believer that predestined signs guided his life journey, and in this case, literally. The first sign read, *Venetian Tacos Ahead*, the next, *Jupiter Enchiladas Ahead*, until the final sign revealed a Mexican restaurant.

Marchia didn't participate in our sessions, but clearly this story tickled both, as she laughed hysterically in the background.

"I'm not making this up, so I pull in there with Jolly and the kids, and here's a Mexican guy out in front of his restaurant, right on Highway 101, and he's got two doors that are swinging doors wide open and flaming torches on each side. And as I approach, he steps forth, he goes, welcome to my establishment, and Mama Sita, get some tortillas for them right away...and he's got this big, wonderful Mexican woman making tortillas by hand over the fire right there in the front of his restaurant. And he welcomes us in, he's such a personality, my god, and he serves a meal, I can't believe it's so delicious. And so what did I say to him? If I gave you a call in a few months, is there any chance you would pick up and come over to Hawaii and make Mexican food there? And the guy says, 'I'm on it let's go'."

Fast forward back to Kaua'i where Gail tells Tom she's decided to sell her restaurant to tie the knot.

"...well, I got a guy that might buy it, so I call Jose, or whatever his name was, and I call him up and I remind him of who I was, and he remembers...and I said I can get this restaurant for five-thousand dollars, and it's got everything, are you interested? He says absolutely, I'll come over in three weeks and look at it. So, Gail is just peeing her pants. she is so excited, her dream is gonna come true. And then Jose doesn't come, and weeks go by, then a few months go by, and she's dying on the vine. Finally, he shows up with four-hundred dollars, after smashing his car while on a trip to Mexico City to say goodbye to his mother before leaving for Hawaii. And to show his sincerity, he shows up with his cook...he left his restaurant in Oxnard...it turns out he's

been run out of town for having hookers and selling cocaine out of the restaurant."

Tom really wants to make this deal happen, not for financial gain, but more his love of Mexican food, so he makes a low-ball offer of one-thousand dollars, and surprisingly she accepts.

"So for one-thousand bucks, I bought the Mexican restaurant, with all the frying pans, a stove, and a fantastic electric tortilla machine that could take any kind of flour and turn it into bits of wonderful tortillas on a flour, corn or anything…and I'm talking about partnerships, and Jose says, we don't need no partnerships, all we want is a straight five dollars an hour each, I couldn't believe it."

Jolly added her artistic creativity, adding authentic flaming tiki torches, while Tom and the crew worked on polishing and cleaning. Opening night was an enormous success, as the place was packed with customers seeking incredible Chili Relleno, wonderful food and reasonable prices. Tom flipped the restaurant for five thousand dollars, turning his opportunistic impetuous nature into a monetary windfall, just by picking wild avocados.

This was one of Tom's favorite stories, reminding him of fun-loving times. I enjoyed the story for varied reasons, as it provided a window into Tom's personality and resourcefulness. Throughout his life, Tom felt a celestial pull leading him towards unique opportunities. Few would spin plucking wild avocados into financial gain, just by following a few Burma signs, but most aren't Tom Morey. Besides, financial gain wasn't his driving force, rather the simple desire to enjoy Mexican food while helping strangers, an emerging pattern that would consistently play out throughout his life.

Tom never gave up on his pursuit to influence surfboard innovation, as evidenced by his six-page "Space Boards" article in the 1971 edition of Surfer magazine. Alongside Tom's spiritual exploration, he never stopped tinkering with way-out design ideas, or as us normal folks called it, spacey. This article had various elements of his boogie idea, notably eliminating the skeg, but he just hadn't pieced it all together.

"The article was a game changer article, nobody had made anything like that, nobody targeted the surfboard shape, the basic shape very much, and I did. I looked at the rails, the sides of the board, and thought well, they don't need to be shaped like they were, they could have a lot of variations in there that suck water to them, and suck the board to the water, instead of having to have this skeg down, this vertical stabilizer all the time…maybe do it with the rails. I had no plan of making the boogie board at that point, but I did have a scheme for making a particular board that's in that article that would suck to the wave, and the air lubrication was another aspect of how to go faster."

Tom's motivation wasn't on building wealth, it was creating wave riding devices aimed at bringing together people of all kinds in the beach playground. Personal finances were erratic, with savings typically supporting material for prototypes, and he always had foam laying around to support his inventive habit (lucky for us).

His studies finally affirmed his belief that ancient religious superstitions, prejudices, and embellished old laws were not natural, but rather exaggerated hype. Although, there was a religious camp more in line with his worldly views and destiny, the Bahá'í faith, delivering not only a new way of life, but also acting as matchmaker for his soulmate of 50 years, Marchia.

Marchia was also a free spirit, surfer, and beach lover. The island community of Kaua'i was small, and Tom remembered a few chance encounters washing sand off their feet and hanging out with friends. Tom had formed a Hawaiian jazz band trio, and named it Uranium, playing gigs at the historic Poipu Beach Hotel, one of the oldest hotels on the Garden Isle. Uranium played three nights a week with each band member getting fifty-bucks per night, enough to supplement the family while allowing Tom to continue with board designs.

On an off night, he headed over to Plantation Gardens restaurant setting up a second chance encounter, where Marchia was a sous chef.

"...there was a very foxy, blond waitress that I was pursuing, and I remember pursuing her into the kitchen for some reason...and there was Marchia in there cooking. And Marchia is one of these girls like

Lily Tomlin that sticks her tongue out and touches the tip of her nose. And so there's Marchia in there with her cooking face on, and I just kind of looked at her and thought...interesting..."

Throughout Tom's research, he attended firesides and devotional meetings discussing the Bahá'í teachings, eventually deciding the beliefs aligned with his new life path. The tenets included the oneness of mankind, universal peace upheld by a world government, independent investigation of truth, the common foundation of all religions, the essential harmony of science and religion, equality of men and women, elimination of prejudice of all kinds, universal compulsory education, a spiritual solution to economic problems, and a universal auxiliary language.

It was during a meeting of the local assembly of Kōloa, unbeknownst to Tom, where Marchia was also being welcomed into the Bahá'í community.

"...and I looked at her across the room, and I was thunderstruck, whatever would be the terms...I just had this thought, it was overwhelming, you have to marry that person or else your life is worthless...I'm on the edge of crying, right now...that's the one, you gotta marry that one, that's it...the relationship went BAM from there."

Their love was instantaneous and genuine. He'd finally found a soulmate he understood, and in return, Marchia embraced Tom's quirky, but loveable nature. They both had a commonality accepting the Bahá'í faith, and unlike Jolly,

Marchia defended Tom's sense of adventure, playfulness, nonconformity, and drive to innovate the surfing world. She was the key to unlocking Tom's transformation from board thumper to ethereal thinker, leading towards purity of life, and she was willing to accept chasing the next big thing, without lasting financial security.

Tom moved out of the house with Jolly and moved into a friend's house with Marchia, while continuing his gig at the Poipu Beach Hotel, until one day a knock on the door sent them on their journey towards boogie fame.

"She (Jolly) wanted to get divorced so that she and her new boyfriend could take possession of the property. I had given her my half of the property for the kids...our divorce was simply about a three-hundred-pound barefoot Hawaiian sheriff entering the place where Marchia and I were living, and served me my papers, ya know, it was almost funny. It was an amicable divorce...I said to her, you have custody, no problem...I'm taking my surfboards...and you can have everything else, and you're in charge of the kids...and I'm going off with this other woman to start a new life and a new way...because she didn't want to go along when it came to the Bahá'í faith, she said, 'Tommy, I've gone along on enough of your trips, I'm over it'."

Tom's memory of the next few months was sketchy. Piecing together his life was a major undertaking, and occasionally we'd hit a gap in the timeline, although his graphic detail of events was impressive. His best recollection was leaving Kaua'i and heading to O'ahu, where he secured his union card playing professionally for the Royal Hawaiian Band, as well as the Honolulu symphony.

The early development of the boogie board began while on Oʻahu, as Tom began building a surfing device he dreamed up from his Spacey article for Surfer magazine. It was designed to surf lying down, and had molded concave sections on the deck, which you could get into and ride with swim fins.

"I had lofted it from 50 pieces of foam that went crosswise that was glued together, and then I shaped one down per my drawings, and had sanded it down with a finish coat of stuff for a covering on this thing, and I tried to surf it out in Waikiki, and a wave came up only three or four inches high, and it snapped the nose off... and it galvanized me to the importance of being able to really hold on to the front of the board and the surfer himself being the foundation and strength of the thing."

By this time, Marchia was pregnant, and both were living in a Volkswagen van. Tom needed to figure out a suitable living arrangement, so he called an old friend, Christel Forth.

"We left Kauaʻi and went to Oʻahu and lived in a Volkswagen van for quite a few months. And then she was getting real pregnant, and so I wanted to get some kind of a place for her, and I had a friend who I had met, Christel Forth, she was the wife of Dove Forth, who was a surfer who I met years earlier in Puerto Rico...and we were all friends, and I called up and said, I'm thinking about coming over to the Big

Island, and she said right away, well come live with me…I'd love to have you come."

Tom packed up their belongings, including the Dow polyethylene ethafoam, and moved to Kailua-Kona, where his first order of business was to marry Marchia in a simple ceremony at the City of Refuge under a palm tree, a stark contrast to his first grandiose wedding.

Christel's house was the perfect location for the boogie inspiration, closely situated to the beach at Wai'aha, commonly referred to as Honl's, the perfect proving grounds located just steps away from her front yard.

Tom gave the design another unsuccessful try before radically re-engineering it.

"I got rid of all the shape that I had, all those cross-sectional curvatures, and that enabled me to level down into the depth. It was a thicker board, it was about six inches thick, and it had a double concave on the bottom…and I got it down to just the plank, and it's just about four feet long, and I realize I can iron it and shape it. I decided to shape the front part roundish and make it a little longer than a foot across so I can hold on to it, and then the back, I curved it down to take the sharp edge off so it wouldn't be a problem against my stomach. I left the bottom trailing edge sharp so that the water would break right off minimizing drag. Then the sides, it intuitively seemed to make sense to make it narrower in the front than the back. I shaped each rail differently… with different curvatures…I'll get better data from that. I shaped the rails more like a boat, where the bottom of the

boat is narrower than the top of the boat, so I beveled the side down like a forty-five-degree angle."

One crucial decision was whether to cut the nine-foot ethafoam blanks in half, or in thirds, experimenting with two or three. He decided on two, but four and a half feet felt too awkward, both wide and long. Tom's initial vision wasn't spot on, but he could feel the burning desire, constructing several more improved prototypes with different shapes, adding longitudinal grooves and ridges for the water to break away, shortening his planks, and improving his ironing technique.

Tom went into the neighbor's trash and pulled out a copy of the July 7, 1971, Honolulu Advertiser, using it as a sample to test on a block of ethafoam. He then snagged Marchia's iron and played with the various heat settings, dialing in exactly how much heat and sweeping motions were necessary to seamlessly melt the paper into the foam. The newspaper was originally applied to buffer Marchia's iron from the melting foam, but surprisingly it adhered, and much to his relief, the foam never melted to the bottom of Marchia's iron. Once he perfected his technique, he used an electric carving knife to shape the freshly cut planks with his design improvements and ironed the boards into wave riding history.

Over the years the story has taken on many variations, including the exact date, since the Honolulu Advertiser was taken out of the trash, and not necessarily on the day he completed the board.

Tom took the device to the Honl's proving ground and confirmed his belief, the board provided a fantastic wave riding experience, maneuverable, durable, cheaply manufactured, lightweight, safe, and fun in all types of waves, especially breakers not surfable with traditional surfboards. Tom rolled off the board onto his knees, ankle deep in water gazing into the heavens thinking, *"I really think this could be something."* Tom ran back to the house and grabbed Marchia, encouraging her to test it. At eight months pregnant, she rode it in on a small wave and enthusiastically gave her stamp of approval.

Not to waste material, he also made a mini version, which he sold for ten dollars to one lucky kid.

"So I made a couple scrap things, and a kid stopped me in the water...and he says, 'you wanna sell one of those things,' I said sure, he said, 'how much you want?', I said, ten bucks...I just pulled a number out of the air...he said, 'great'."

That first sale inspired confidence that the newly created wave riding device had commercial viability, and validated Tom's imaginative journey. Tom couldn't remember what happened to the first board, but the second board I consider an historic treasure that should be displayed in the Smithsonian.

Stories surrounding the boogie name became folklore, perpetuated mostly by Morey himself, although Tom admitted, after fifty years of storytelling, even he couldn't keep up with the embellishment of events. Depending on what you read, and where you read it, a few variations exist, each revolving around a Bahá'í prayer, commonly referred to as the rose garden prayer. One variation, or a combination of all, has Tom reciting the prayer the night before shaping the blank, another has Tom reciting the prayer while dreaming of ancient Polynesian Pacific islanders surfing wooden paipo boards designed to slide across the ocean swells lying down, and yet another naming the device SNAKE from previous prayer sessions.

Tom reveals the real story is more pragmatic than one might think. Christel Forth was a lovely petite, cigarette smoking, separated German girl who worked at a local restaurant and sewed bikinis for extra money.

"I was trying to be a vegetarian...she'd come home with leftover roast beef, steak, and lobsters and I would feed it to the dogs...I'd hear about that man."

Between Marchia, Christel and her two red setters, quiet time was at a premium, and Tom was simply looking for space to meditate and conduct his Bahá'í rituals, the closet seemed like a good place to get away from all the noise and distractions. That's where his creative thought provided a multitude of answers throughout his boogie conception.

The device had already been shaped, ironed, tested and initially named the SNAKE Machine, returning to his love of acronyms, but the side, navel, arm, knee and elbow, wasn't getting favorable reviews.

"I went with side, naval, arm, knee, and elbow, the snake machine, because my name was Morey and there was a moray eel, and the materials feel like an eel, and I was going to go with that somehow, and put Morey and eel together…then I tried out SNAKE Machine and one person said, 'I don't like snakes', another said 'snakes are from the devil'."

Tom ultimately, whether consciously or through divine intervention, drew from his love of music, mixing together the hottest dance music of his time (Boogie Woogie), with the playfulness of surfing, creating the historied name, Boogie Board. He added the name Morey as an homage to his father's real estate business.

"I started working on the name Morey, and the calligraphy of that, and that's because my dad had band sawed some wooden letters that spelled Morey for a sign hanging out for his real estate business."

Tom loved Hawaii for its spirit, island music and surfing heritage, but the business of California was calling him back to the mainland. His motivation was now tapping into foam suppliers and manufacturing partnerships, but first he had to deal with his meager financial situation. Tom's good fortune continued, when the local Bahá'í Chairman, Jack Spark, saw his boogie and graciously gifted him two hundred dollars. With that, Tom was able to sell his car and scrape together enough cash for him and Marchia to return to Pasadena, where he had an open invitation to stay with his best USC buddy, Bob Tierney. Marchia's parents, whom Tom had never met, also provided a much-needed lift by delivering a used 1949 Chrysler automobile as a belated wedding present.

The initial plan wasn't to build the boards himself, but to partner with a manufacturer selling the boogie concept for royalties. After several months of failed attempts, things were getting desperate. At thirty-seven years old, Tom was a father once again, and funds were exhausted. As a last-ditch effort, Tom arranged a meeting with G&S Surfboards, Larry Gordon and Floyd Smith, showcasing his newspaper ironed foam board contraption.

"…it was a cold dreary day at Pacific Beach, and I pull up and there's this sales guy, kind of a wiseass kid (laughing) and I pull this thing out of the trunk of the car…and we suit up with our wetsuits, and we're wading out in the cold, and this wiseass sales manager turns to Floyd and Larry and says, 'Guys, I don't think you could sell these things for three dollars'…and this guy loves to tell that story…Balsa Bill Yerkes, who's a dear friend…so we go out there and Floyd and Larry can see the thing works…so we then go back to the shop and I propose a deal…"

As I continued to quiz Tom on this wiseass sales manager, I discovered Balsa Bill Yerkes lived near me in Cocoa Beach, Florida, operating a surf shop still making custom

Balsa boards. Bill was also a talented musician, playing a multitude of instruments, including ukulele, piano and guitar. In fact his Beach Boys cover band, The Surf Chasers, is a family affair, and Bill is old friends with The Beach Boys, having authored several books photo documenting their 1966 tour.

This was the one and only time when Tom contacted a collaborator and offered me the opportunity to call Bill directly, and I'm thankful I did. Bill was the sales manager for G&S travelling along the coast and taking orders from all the surf shops, but on this momentous day, Yerkes happened to be in town when Morey showed up with the boogie.

"And so Tom shows up…and says to Larry, 'I want to show you something,' so Larry motions to me and says, 'come on, Bill', and Tom turns around and says, 'who's he?'…Larry replies, 'this is Bill, he's my sales guy'. So we went out to the car, and Tom had a '49 Chrysler business coupe. And a business coupe was designed back in those days for traveling salesman, and they had a short little cockpit, and one front seat, no back seat, it was a coupe, and it had this giant long trunk where a salesman could carry samples…the things running because if he shuts it off, he can't start it again…and so this car is sitting there running…and he pops the trunk…and we said, what's this?. And he said, 'I call this a boogie board, and you can ride waves with it'… So Larry turns to me and says, 'What do you think we can sell them for?', and Tom chimes in, 'We can retail them for thirty

bucks.' I said thirty, I don't think they'll sell for three dollars. I was wrong, Tom was right."

Tom finally found a trusted manufacturing partner with a mutual commitment towards developing a saleable product. The deal included five percent of gross sales (less returns and discounts), advanced royalties, good faith effort to utilize available G&S resources, one-hundred-and-eighty dollars weekly salary and use of the company truck. Tom also requested five hundred dollars, cash, so he could take something home to satisfy Marchia. Larry had enormous respect for Tom's design talent, so as part of the deal, Larry asked Tom to design custom surfboards, which led to the famed G&S WaterSkate.

One day in 1972, Tom wanted to design a board, so he headed to Balsa Bill's small beach front apartment at Mission Beach and asked Bill if he had the key to the G&S factory. Luckily, he did. The WaterSkate was inspired by Vinny Byran's design, a surfer/shaper who made a few plywood paipo (bellyboards) as a youth, surfing them on the shore break at Makaha in the 1950's, and continuing with surfboard designs throughout the 1960's from his Central Coast Surf Shop located in the San Luis Obispo area.

Balsa Bill Yerkes continues with the story.

"So he was talking about different designs, and he was talking about some designs that a guy named Vinny Byran was doing in Hawaii, and they were big thick short boards…and whether anyone was doing

those on the east coast...and he thought they'd be a perfect board for the East Coast, I agreed. So there was a blank in there for a lifeguard board, a twelve foot long blank, so Tom takes this twelve-foot-long blank, cause it was big and thick, you know, and he cut it down to a six foot board...and it had high rails on one side, and dished out in the center, oh it was spacey looking, and to me it was very commercial since I was the guy that had to go out and sell these...so I shot it with my telephoto lens and showed it to Gordon and said make me one of these and send me back to the East Coast...I gotta sell something."

After I spoke with Balsa Bill, I called Tom to add some more color to the story, in fact, all sorts of colors.

"I developed a surfboard that was a sensational board...and I called it the WaterSkate, and in the ad it was the first and only surfboard that had a concave deck, it had the deck scooped up quite a bit, so you can lie in it comfortably, and be nuzzled in there and also when you stood on the board, if you picture how you stand on a surfboard, with its rounded top which is convex, and the WaterSkate had a concave deck, and the concave goes beautifully with how your feet actually stand on the rail and stand on the board. So this board was cool, good looking, and I prescribed that they must color these boards a certain way to make them stand out from other boards...these boards are gonna be a solid color; solid purple, solid yellow, solid black, solid blue..."

Floyd and Larry bought into the concept directing Tom to switch away from lifeguard blanks, which were cost prohibitive, and to make it more in line with current market demands.

Shortly after the launch of the WaterSkate, Tom caught another break, as his divorce struck an administrative snag.

"Jolly, who I had left the ranch to, fell for a guy, and wanted to get married. And the fact that I was still on the deed with the property on Kaua'i, encumbered her plans. She and this guy wanted to have a clean bill of sale. So we sat and talked, and I figured out what the price was that I paid, and a profit...I paid forty two five, and by then I figure well, it's probably worth fifty two five, cuz it's not going up very fast, so you give me half of that (twenty-six thousand, two hundred and fifty), and I'll sell you my half of it."

Not only was Tom back in the game financially, but he figured out a key manufacturing step, leading him to mutually part ways with G&S, effectively cancelling the licensing deal in exchange for Tom's WaterSkate creation. In essence, he took back the boogie and gave G&S the WaterSkate. It wasn't for lack of effort from G&S, but rather not finding suitable skin material during the development phase, which included failing with different types of paints, priming materials, contact cement, and heat wielding applications.

Finding the final piece to the puzzle was strictly chance, or was it? Either way the timing was perfect.

"And finally, one day I went back to the distributor of my foam (Wilshire Foam Factory), and I saw he had another similar foam...and they were skiving off the tops and bottoms...the crust of the foam buns they mold...and they were just trashing these skins,

from this kind of foam. This was L200 mini foam, Taiwanese foam. So I saw all those skins, and I went over with my fingernail to scratch at it, and feel it on my chest, and it had quite a bit of durability, and it was slick, and it had a very unusual and interesting pattern in that it was blemished, and I imagined this on the boogie, and that this thing could look damn good. So I asked them for a bunch of skins…and I figured out that I could contact cement those skins to the polyethylene core, one on the top, and one on the bottom, and that made it possible to make the boogie."

With the financial windfall, Tom and Marchia bought a home on Chestnut Street in Carlsbad, supplementing income with drumming gigs, while fully committing to developing a manufacturing process transitioning the boogie board to a fully finished and marketable product.

Not only did he commandeer Marchia's kitchen table, but the entire property became a mini-manufacturing facility, filled with solvent, resin, cement, foam, skins, and various appliances. Tom's expertise as a process engineer rose to the forefront as he began to figure out how to assemble a quality, good looking, finished Boogie Board. The process was laborious, including several steps, cutting, sanding, skinning, cementing, drying, glueing, drying, trimming, all while dealing with solvent fumes and wind-blown leaves sticking to the tacky boards drying on the hedges and driveway.

"…and so you had to squeeze around all this thick resin, and fumes are coming off like crazy, and it's a mess, and it's not drying uniformly

and all this stuff. And then set it out in the sun so it'll dry and wait till it's right and then stick it together without the wind or leaves or something causing problems…and then squeeze it together with my hand with a 7UP bottle that I would roll back and forth and hope the hell I got enough pressure and that there was enough solvent out of all of this, so it didn't swell up and delaminate, all this kind of stuff."

Tom's tenacity finally paid off powering through headaches, rashes and respiratory issues successfully constructing a cool, sexy, fun, marketable, prone riding device now aptly named, the Morey Boogie Board. The next challenge, launch a marketing and advertising plan and hope for the best. Tom's earlier advertising and promotion experience from Morey-Pope Surfboards provided a foundation for revealing the Boogie, but it required some updating, so he headed down to the San Diego library, and found the perfect advertising vehicle, mail order.

"I then went to the San Diego Library, and I went into the stacks, I looked up mail order advertisement and I found a book that was thin and appealed to me…I took it home and devoured it and based on that…I wrote a really good…I call it a slice and dice ad…and I chose thirty-seven dollars for the price of the board, because I was thirty-seven years old. It seemed like a good number…as the cost (to make it) was under ten bucks."

Tom grabbed Marchia with her camera and headed down to a surf break in La Jolla, where she shot a picture of the boogie zipping down a fun wave. With that picture, and Tom's creative advertising copy, they produced the first

Morey Boogie Board mail order advertisement, which was placed in Surfer Magazine. The advertisement had a dotted-line cutout with an area requesting a check, and room to insert the purchasers' return mail address.

All Tom could do now was wait.

"I'd walk out to the mailbox slowly and walk around the box a couple of times and then look in….nothing. One day I looked in there, and there was one little envelope, not a full-size envelope, but a smaller one, and in this kind of youthful handwriting was my address, and I opened that, and stupid me, I did not save that one…my first customer, the first to believe. And so the next day I look in there, there's five, next day, nothing, next day, three, next day one, and it went on like that, until it was pretty clear that this was going to sell. Because if it was not going to sell, I'm gonna just send the checks back and call it a day…but it did sell."

A steady stream of orders rolled in, but keeping up with hand-assembled manufacturing was becoming an issue, not only that, but Tom's health was slowly worsening from the toxic mix of solvents and foam. Tom decided to abandon the finished manufacturing process and develop a kit with detailed, handwritten, step by step instructions and illustrations, all penned by Tom himself. The kit was an improved version of the original, with a reduced price of twenty-five dollars, and included a hand-shaped polyethylene core, razor blade, sandpaper, roll off edge tape and two large smooth dimpled iridescent boogie skins, the customers only had to purchase the glue and brush.

The handwritten instructions are a fabulous read, and I highly recommend you jump online and search "history of the Boogie Board." You'll find plenty of websites showcasing the Morey Boogie legacy, or better yet, stop by the California Surf Museum, located in Oceanside, California, where you'll find the Morey Boogie exhibit. The four-page instruction manual, in my opinion, is one of Tom's best written works, easily understood and entertaining.

One interesting fact I never clarified with Tom from the kit advertisement was the mention of alternative purchase options, including Rich Parr, Honolulu, Mother Nature's Son, Kōloa and Joan Rochelle, Kapaa. The copy mentions "while materials last," and I'm speculating he set up Hawaiian mail order supply options based on acquaintances while living in Hawaii, but it's one nagging detail I let slip through the crack and never confirmed with Tom. The fact that the advertisement states, "while materials last" would support his next evolution into a small warehouse located on Oak Street, across from the Boys and Girls Club, where he abandoned kits and transitioned back to assembling a finished product for wholesale distribution.

SESSION SIX - TRADEMARK REGRET

Tom and Marchia were now working hard as a team travelling with board samples and invoice books selling a dozen at a time to local surf shops building the Morey Boogie brand from the ground up. From a marketing perspective, Tom applied the same principles from the surfboard industry to the Boogie Board, holding tryouts for Boogie surf teams and staging local competitions, cultivating a distinctive Boogie tribe.

The discontinued mail order revenue, combined with ongoing wholesale transactions afforded enough cash to hire their first significant employee, Bobby Szabad.

"…my first guy that was of any consequence was Bobby Szabad, and Bobby comes on, and he's a good-looking guy, and a good surfer, and he's steadfast, and he right away brings in his pal, Rick Broderson. And Bobby also brings in the Szabad's, he's got his father, his mother and his brother, Frank, and some other Hawaiians, cause Oceanside is sort of a Hawaiian settlement."

Tom's love of surfboard design led to his next collaborator, Mike Doyle. Doyle was a showman on the liquid stage, and while working with Tom in 1974, created the first soft surfboard. Doyle was an artist and innovator, whose primary focus was on the surfboard business.

"Mike Doyle came along...putting a single stringer in the foam...with plenty of stiffness, but allowed for side to side...torsional flexibility...and he made the skeg be part of the stringer..."

Happenstance with a local neighborhood kid, Craig Libuse, led to the Morey Boogie's first hair-blending, wave flowing iconic logo.

"...well, back in the kit days, we were living there in Carlsbad, only two blocks from the ocean, and there's a pretty good spot, right there at the end of our street. And we had some local kids that got hot...well the local kids were comprised of the first team, which was Tepe Paul, Jr., Allen French, Matt Norton, and Tepe's little kid brother...the original surf team. Then along comes Libuse, he comes by the place one day, and he had made a kit he wanted to show me, so I said, let me see your kit. Well, he was a very clean cut, good looking, young man...a real man, you know, and his wife was a fox...and sure enough, he shows me this kit he made, and man, it was perfect, it was better than anything I was making (laughing)...this guy had craftsmanship and I talked about what he did and his father was a prototype builder of woodworking things, and Craig was an artist and dabbled in prototypes. So I'm gonna need a logo, so I ask him, do you wanna take a crack at this? Sure. So, we have a picture of Tepe riding, and he sees that picture, and we loan him some pictures and show him things...Tepe had this long hair...so he comes up with a logo of Tepe, with the long hair flowing back into the wave...it was gorgeous man,

cool...so I bought the rights, and I paid him some good money...twenty-five dollars."

Libuse was eventually hired as art director, imprinting his lasting artistic signature on the Morey Boogie advertisements and overall brand.

The Morey Boogie phenomenon was exploding, and the Oak Street warehouse simply wasn't providing enough space, forcing a relocation to the nearby, five-thousand-square-foot Roosevelt Street manufacturing facility.

Tom never anticipated the Morey Boogie to be a big deal, and managing the business outpaced Tom's experience to cope with manufacturing, employee acquisition and escalating sales. Tom turned to "Up the Organization, How to Stop Management from Stifling People and Strangling Productivity," a New York Times bestselling book by Robert Townsend, published in 1970, to glean advice on corporate culture. Townsend was the CEO who successfully transformed Avis's car rental company through implementing a management style designed to humanize the business, thereby bringing out the best in people by getting out of their way. It was the perfect management approach for Tom, allowing him freedom to focus on new creative endeavors, which led to his next hire and business partner, Germaine Jim Faivre.

"...I couldn't do this alone, and we kept coming across this guy...he was broke and he was a recovering alcoholic, he was a wonderful spirit,

he had been a bum on the tracks, many times…over many years, and previous to that, he had been a foreman on construction crews in Puerto Rico, building hospitals…at some point he had as many as 2000 men under him. He was quite a fabulous character, but he's not like some guy that puffs his chest out like some executive, he's sort of a guy that you would see in a swash buckling movie, and very well loved by his cohorts and employees, he just had natural pizazz…he was dedicated to his own kind of cause, I don't know what it was, but it was alcohol and knife sharpening…and he would go on a toot, out to the hobo camp, and go in to town and go to the markets…get vegetables and buy outdated fruits and make a stew at the hobo camp and drink…then sober up and come back to work…he drank maybe seven or eight cups of black coffee, with three spoonful's of sugar in each cup…always had a cigarette going…and he loved to make knives, he'd find a piece of metal and turn it into a knife and grind it down and had the magnifying glasses, and a cup of coffee…and he was happy."

Jim Faivre's main allure was his aptitude for carpentry, tooling, and heat welding, and with business exploding, Tom needed someone to help him figure out a swift production process to keep up with demand, finally devising a way to efficiently cut the foam and heat-weld the deck to the core.

On Thursday, August 7, 1975, Tom Morey and Co., Inc. filed an application for the Morey Boogie word mark with the United States Patent and Trademark office, US Serial Registration number 73059986, for the category listed as, "flexible, lightweight, buoyant polyethylene foam surfing device for use in riding waves in a prone position". The first use date listed was October 7, 1973, and the first use in commerce date was October 14, 1973. Those dates roughly correspond to sales made while working out of the residence at Chestnut Street. The granted registration date was September 14, 1976.

Tom wasn't a big fan of protectionism, and felt discoveries and inventions should be open for everyone to enjoy, without commercial gain, but in this case Tom's gut was telling him otherwise, and he was wise to listen. His dream of introducing an affordable wave riding device to the masses was about to be fulfilled, unbeknownst to him, beyond his wildest expectations.

"We finally had plenty of manufacturing space and we had our heat welder, and we had three shifts, and we had about sixty employees at our peak, and we had another forty in Mexico, we had one hundred employees, and we were not making good use of them at all. We had three facilities, two of them running twenty-four hours a day...then we went to J.C. Penny's, and Sears Roebuck, Neiman Marcus, Gimbels, and everybody...the boards were selling for twenty-five dollars wholesale, and we were making one thousand boards a day."

My typical routine was to review our conversations each night, outlining story points I felt required a deeper dive, or clarification of facts. At times, Tom would jokingly muddle a few facts, testing my fact checking diligence. Throughout our journey, he had a knack of sporadically assessing my ability to get the story straight. Other times it was clearly a momentary lapse in memory; most times he was spot on. In this case I circled back to the Mexico facility and daily output of boards. Tom couldn't remember the exact output figures and vacillated between one thousand and one hundred boards daily. I finally located an August 24,1978, San Diego Reader article entitled "Boogie boards got their start in Carlsbad" by Gordon Smith, pegging the sales between four to eight hundred per day, at its peak, and one hundred per day at the Oak Street location. Whatever the actual number, it was a good chunk of change.

I then zeroed in on the Mexico facility, hoping he hadn't opened the factory for his love of Mexican food. The answer turned out to be both altruistic and disheartening, but consistent with Tom's propensity to service others, while minimizing the importance of fiduciary responsibility.

It seems an unforeseen consequence of banging out boatloads of Boogie Boards is mounds of leftover foam, which led to a series of serendipitous events.

"And we had a mound of scrap foam that was the size of your house, I haven't seen your house, but every room in your house absolutely full to the ceiling, plus your neighbor's house, and with a thousand boards a week…a day…getting made, it was a lot of scrap. Independent of that, I had a Bahá'í friend, Max Taylor. He came in the door one day and he had made an airplane out of scrap foam. And it was a two-by-two inch wide and high strip of foam about forty inches long, that was heat welded using the same technology we used to weld the boards together. He had made his version of the SST (Mach 2

Supersonic Transport)…and he made a thing that you could throw across the room…it went pretty good, and it was kind of fun."

Tom began making and selling a few SSTs through the shop, but couldn't resist the urge to make improvements, figuring out how to dye the foam with marking pen ink and silk screens with red, white, and blue patterns. In the meantime, Jim Faivre had formed some business dealings in El Rosario de Arriba, Baja California, which resulted in a Mexican facility for scrap planes.

"Jim was going down there (El Rosario de Arriba) on weekends, helping out and camping down there helping a lot of poor people…and he was sort of pioneering some kind of a business down there, so we were paying around one dollar an airplane, something like that to assemble them and paint them, and pretty soon we had a pretty good sized crew, and we were making quite a few of these airplanes. Now, our sales were not keeping up with it, and this was a doomed plan, because, as it turns out, it's not a good idea to start using scrap materials for a product, because sooner or later you come out of balance, and you have to start buying materials because you don't have enough scrap or, you have so much scrap and it keeps piling up…so we trampled ourselves with that thing."

This was just one of several poor business decisions self-inflicted due to Tom's inventive addiction. Tom kept pursuing the next big thing, and most of his inventions were solid ideas, simply way ahead of their time without adequate capital, including the Morey Boogie Land Waterpark. Each time I mentioned one of his inventive ideas, Tom exploded with excitement, like a faucet that just kept flowing.

"Oh my God, oh my God, Ok…one day a Frenchman comes in the door…it's very exciting to be telling this kind of stuff…the shop is a very exciting place…you have all these characters and you have all this romance going on in the background…and you have youth coming of age and coming into the shop, and embracing causes and all this stuff is fun, fun, fun. Now this Frenchman comes in and speaks with a very thick accent, and he wants to try and get a free Boogie Board from us because he has developed this standing water-skiing deal, and what he has is an impeller that is sucking water from the bottom of a ramp. He's got a ramp about six or eight feet wide, and twelve or fifteen feet long, plywood, and at the bottom of this, he's got blowers that are spinning water from what gathers at the bottom, spinning and thrusting water up this ramp. And then you can hold onto a rope and have a water-skiing experience going down this ramp with the water coming up it. So he wanted to try with a boogie board. So we got him a boogie board and we looked at his film of what he had actually built, then I commandeered Craig Libuse to render Boogie Land based on my vision of a waterpark."

The contraption was the early basis for the FlowRider Wave Machine, and Tom's waterpark vision predated Kelly Slaters Surf Ranch by 30 years.

Six years after his Boogie creation on The Big Island, Tom Morey and Co., Inc. was churning out thousands of boards monthly while generating millions of dollars in topline sales annually, including Doyle Soft Boards. Balsa Bill Yerkes earlier assessment of the Boogie Board was partially correct. The rapid popularity of the Boogie Board was due to its perception as a toy or novelty item, effectively replacing the inflatable surf mat. This viewpoint greatly impacted the Boogie Board becoming a family water sport necessity when heading out to enjoy the waves.

That is until Patti Serrano, the most powerful organizer and promoter in Boogie Boarding history, came along.

"So Patti comes over, and she's got a natural gift for gab and promotion and joy of being on the scene and seeing the young guys…she's like a natural youth leader, you know, and she really has a great love for a lot of people and gets them stoked up and so she's a natural to promote this thing…"

Prior to Serrano, Marchia and Tom would hold local competitions in Carlsbad, serving hot chocolate at the beach, judging Boogie Board heats and awarding prizes.

"And that was fun, just a lot of fun. We had some kind of prizes and trophies. And once you started hosting some events, everybody loves to be involved and have the competition and people really embrace a new activity, God, imagine coquette or basketball and all that, just starting up, you know."

It was Patti's tenacity, high energy, and love for Boogie Boarding that helped formulate an entirely new sport. Patti coincidentally met Tom in the 1960s within a small Bahá'í community on the island of Kaua'i. Tom visited her health food bakery, Pat C Pink Breads, after a surf session to enjoy her renowned oatmeal cookies. A second coincidental meeting in Carlsbad led to her hiring, initially doing clerical work. Tom Morey and Co., Inc. was truly a family affair, with Patti bringing her kid sister on board too, Debbie Colwell.

"And she's got a kid sister Debbie. Debbie could use a job…Debbie comes down…so we start Debbie off in shrink wrapping…the final product that's run through the heat shrink plastic coating after the poster is put in there and then she's trimming skins, she's just doing all the grunt work, ya know, like everybody else, and she keeps getting better, and better and better at it…"

With the goal of expanding Boogie Board sales, while simultaneously re-branding away from novelties, Patti crafted a plan for contests sanctioned by the Western Boogie Association, which she established in 1977. She used the WBA as a springboard, creating pro circuits and grassroots beach events to share the joy with beachgoers, tying in consignment sales and pro riders with local surf shops.

In 1978, Tom came to the realization that the business was slipping away from his control. It seemed like déjà vu all over again, flashbacking to his Morey-Pope days where he wanted to escape back to Hawaii. Tom was selling a ton of boards, but struggling with bottom-line profit, in fact, they needed a cash infusion to keep up with operations, and financing was difficult.

"...it became obvious that I didn't want to stay in a partnership, and I also didn't want to be making calls that affected him (Jim Faivre) and all these employees, and I started doubting my own capabilities, I didn't want to keep living in Carlsbad, because we had pioneered and opened up Hawaii, and there was nobody running things over there, and hell, I could go over there and run things. So I called up Marchia one day and I said, how about we move back to Hawaii...she said, 'of course, let's go to Hawaii, what the hell are we doing with all this traffic and smog'."

Out of the blue, Tom got a call from John Rosekrans, and his partner John Bowes, asking about the possible sale of the Boogie Board business. Rosekrans and Bowes had been friends since the fourth grade, and both attended Stanford University, with Bowes securing a master's degree in business from Harvard. In 1963 they founded Kransco, selling floating furniture for swimming pools. Bowes specialty was finding undervalued companies, building them up and selling them for astronomical sums of money. The company's primary mission was to grow through acquisitions, eventually becoming the largest privately owned toy company in the United States, acquiring Wham-O, Hacky Sack, and Power Wheels before selling to Mattel, netting more than three hundred and fifty million dollars.

Timing was perfect for both Morey Boogie and Kransco, as the acquisition aligned with Kransco's newly minted growth strategy, as well as Morey's need for a bailout.

"So they called and asked if I would I be interested in selling? Hell yea, come on down and take a look...so we danced around and went to all these negotiations and finally came up with pricing. And Jim and I were equal partners on a handshake. But these guys kind of laughed behind Faivre's back, because Faivre's a character...he's got a goatee and he's got a van dyke (beard), and he wears a beret slanted on his head, and he's always got a cigarette, and he's not a businessman. These guys prided themselves on their business acumen...so, I got so many hundreds of thousands of dollars down, and they bought so many hundreds of thousands of dollars' worth of goods that were unfinished, and we sold them the tooling...gave them the account list and all that and ferried them all around so they could sell and all that stuff...and made a good transfer."

In exchange for selling the business, Tom received five percent of gross sales on the first two million in sales for a year, and then three percent on the next million for a year, and then two percent on everything over that, which amounted to a decent payout, given the existing financial state of the company. Tom unloaded the continental United States, including Canada, withholding Hawaii, and he split the payout evenly with Jim Faivre.

Tom didn't have many regrets in life. In fact, he loved his storied and colorful past, but the regrets he did have ran deep.

The first was his non-compete clause.

"I signed a never compete, and to not encourage my sons."

My heart sank as Tom articulated the words, "never compete" and "to not encourage my sons."

"...but it's been forty years, and I've stuck with it, however I was stupid in not getting a strong quality assurance paragraph in there, and I assumed they would be gentlemanly and would do the right thing, and so forth."

The second was surrendering the Morey Boogie trademark bearing his family legacy.

"...I forget how I negotiated, but I probably am forgetting because I didn't do it very well. Because as the inventor, I'm thinking, it's just a light bulb, I've got many more inventions coming...I thank God that I'm not still in the boogie board business...I don't even want to say boogie board anymore. I'll say this, we made some good money, we got some good royalties, Kransco paid the bills and took care of business...I have some gripes about things that we didn't cover in the contract initially, where I got stuck for thousands and thousands of dollars...but I don't want to go into that..."

I sensed a resentment in Tom's voice surrounding the sale to Kransco. Bowes and Rosekrans were acquisition specialists, highly competitive, cutthroat business executives specifically focused on finding novelty inventors and pouncing on their struggling businesses, the very antithesis of Tom's foundational beliefs. The negotiation leverage was clearly on the side of Kransco, which is why Tom wiped the trademark concession from his memory banks. The loss of the Morey name cut even deeper given the sentimental connection to his father's real estate business, and the missing quality assurance clause came back to bite him in the ass, as global production shifted towards styrene beads in the mass manufacturing process, which cheapened the boards bearing the Morey Boogie name.

On Monday, May 1, 1978, the trademark office recorded an assignment from Morey and Co., Inc. to Kransco Manufacturing Inc., closing the purchase of Morey Boogie.

Tom hung around for the transition, eventually handing off daily operations to Phil Stubbs. The Kransco culture slowly moved away from an open free-flowing hippy vibe to cautious policies protecting the manufacturing process. They moved from Roosevelt Street to a new Oceanside industrial park and switched the distribution model away from Mom and Pops to larger, more sophisticated operators with greater reach and efficiency. Most importantly, they cracked down on the illegal use of the trademark, trying unsuccessfully to prevent "Boogie" from becoming a generic term, such as, *"grab your boogie and let's head down to the water."* This led to a major shift in boogie boarding terminology, a change that Morey despised. Tom thought the term bodyboarding was stupid, akin to a piece of dead flesh sitting on a slab in the morgue.

The market differentiation was clearly defined. Boogie Boarders were considered beginners, with children and weekend beach goers playing in the waves. Bodyboarders became professional athletes surfing high quality boards on challenging waves with specialized fins, while conducting numerous high-flying maneuvers. Boogie boards could be purchased on the cheap at any drug, grocery, or department store, while bodyboards were purchased from custom-shapers, or professionally endorsed pro riders.

The neighborhood kids once employed by Morey had graduated from his boogie board masterclass, including Bobby Szabad, who went on to form the very successful BZ Bodyboard brand. Debbie Colwell, formed CustomX Bodyboards, and Rick Broderson headed over to New Zealand to begin manufacturing several different brands, including the Morey Boogie. Serrano eventually accepted the position of Sports Promotion Manager for Kransco, later branching out on her own to found Bodyboarder International Magazine (BIM), and the Bodyboarder International Association, which included a recreation division for non-competitors.

SurferToday.com founder Luís Madureira Pinto has created an incredible archive of boogie boarding history complete with vintage advertisements, interviews, photo essays, and the wave pool vison sketched by Craig Libuse, just to name a few. If you're looking for a cultural reference of the times, or vintage photos, check it out.

In the 1980's, the transformation from boogie to bodyboarding was further spearheaded by a bodyboarding phenomenon named, Mike Stewart. He changed the perception of boogie wave riding to big time barrel chasing, pipeline dropping bodyboarding, garnering mutual respect among tribal surfboard communities. He was, and possibly still is, bodyboarding's version of the G.O.A.T. (greatest of all time).

"...and along comes this kid, a phenomenon came along...Michael...Mike Stewart, that was just a nice little kid in some of the early competitions, but with an iron will to win. He kept getting better and better, and the competition of the Boogie Board started having some prize money and it was very interesting to watch because it's done at Bonsai pipeline, which is a hell of a scary big wave that's very close in, and an audience can be there on the beach and see it and hoot and holler, and the cameras are rolling...it's really a photographer's paradise...and that took the Boogie board up for quite a few years, as a major competition, with some pretty good prize money."

Tom's simple dream of bringing together all people to play nice in the beach playground got temporarily reengineered by tribal surf culture, as boogie boarders were named spongers, speed bumps, and dick draggers. It's one of those things where idealistic sports cultures don't like being treaded on by a lesser entity. Maybe it's cultural infringement, or newly crowded breaks, or jealousy, or affordability, or a combination of all. Or maybe they took a cue from Morey's very first advertisement in Surfer with the tagline, "Boogie safely over guys in your way, skim beneath the curl into the shallowest waters or warp yourself into positions no one has yet dreamed of." Whatever it was, the cultural clash was well documented. Just jump on YouTube and search "Surfer vs. Bodyboarder" and you'll get some crazy fights and collision videos on crowded surf breaks. One of my favorites is SURFERS VS. BODYBOARDERS | KOOK BATTLE, from the Life of Kook channel. Eventually, bodyboarding lost the viewership battle as advertising and sponsorship dollars got squeezed, leaving surfing and newly arrived skateboarding surviving the clash.

Tom, Marchia, and the kids set sail back to Hawaii, but not before leaving behind an indelible and historic imprint on the surfing world.

SESSION SEVEN - LOVERS PACT

"...the thing about my life is, there's not much tragedy...underlying all this...I have been especially chosen to do this job, and I have also, once I started getting near the fire of the thing, been strongly praying, striving to get this job done, cuz I am the revealer...Moses goes up and smokes marijuana, and comes down from the burning bush, whatever it is, but Moses comes down and reveals the ten commandments, and Jesus reveals his thing, and Morey doesn't reveal anything that big, but I do happen to be gifted with the revelation of the boogie board, and that's no small deal, it was a small deal and it seemed to be...but it turns out it's a big deal. It really fucking works, man, the thing really works...it's like being gifted with the inflatable tire."

Session seven kicked off with a lot to unpack.

It's the old saying, if I knew then what I know now. Would Tom really make different life decisions? Maybe yes, maybe no, but having regret late in life has a way of messing with your head, almost as much as Tom liked to mess with mine.

I was becoming mesmerized with Tom's charm, humor, wit, and intelligence, as I began discussing the character in our movie, and the importance of success, as well as disappointment. Tom's self-reflection didn't recognize tragedy, even though I felt the sting of selling Morey Boogie to Kransco, and I struggled with what Tom's life might look like if he had hired a competent CEO with solid start up skills to run the show. Then, it hit me, I was self-reflecting on what I wanted for Tom, and not what he wanted for himself, essentially playing the sympathy game. Even though the audience may feel compassion for the character, Tom Morey had accomplished what he set out to do, and was now free to let loose his inner mad scientist. And that's exactly what he did.

Tom and Marchia, now with four boys, spent the next five or so years enjoying the fruits of their labor, purchasing two homes on Hawaii's Big Island, primarily living within the community of Puako, along the Kohala Coast. Tom was living large, occasionally playing music, while letting his imagination run wild with inventive ideas. A May 10, 1982, Sports Illustrated article entitled "The Ocean Speaks to You, but you wouldn't believe the things it tells Tom Morey, the inventor of the Boogie board," by Franz Lidz, describes all sorts of inventions rolling around Tom's brain, including mylar toothpicks, a circular book, an improved football, a sailboat with an adjustable mast, three-player chess, Ping-Pong games, and his futuristic flying contraption, the AirSkate, based on an original idea from Alexander Lippisch and the 1972 Dornier Aerodyne flight.

Tom had been dreaming about the AirSkate since the early 1980's, it was something he wanted badly, up until the end, his next big thing, but could never get financing. He tried to walk me through a paper prototype of the plane, but honestly, I was lost. I concede, I'm usually not the smartest dude in the room, but maybe those more aerodynamically inclined will get it.

"I got interested in something back then, of which I'm still interested in, and I'll tell you about it. If you have a sheet of paper there in front of you, and you fold it lengthwise, right down the middle, and then crease that, and put the two sides together and take the scissors, and then cut from the point of one of this fold, all the way down to the diagonal corner, and you cut both of those at the same time, you should have a triangle that's folded down the middle. You set that on a smooth wood floor, or a table, and it's got a big yawing mouth on one end, and it tapers down to nothing at the other end. So if you then just leave it on the table, it's sort of like a section of a roof, and it's stable. Now put a couple of paper clips on the open end, the wide end, for weight, and you give it a little push from the tail, it kind of lifts up in the air a little bit, and it would go across the floor a little ways…and if you had a rudder in the back that sticks up in the air, the thing will slide quite a ways along the floor, maybe five or ten feet."

Tom was clearly channeling his inner engineering professor, as the next several minutes focused on his tutelage of dihedral, and his view of manipulating wing tips with anhedral for his AirSkate. Tom continually improved the concept, first transitioning from paper to thicker file folders, then Scramble Stix, eventually graduating to a twelve-foot fiberglass model powered with an outboard motor, him sitting on the front edge, while zipping across calm waters. Next was a thirty-footer with a pusher propeller, retracting wheels, and a fifty-five horsepower Volkswagen engine.

I asked Tom what his goal was. Was the AirSkate to be commercialized and used for transportation?

"Well, don't you ever do anything without having a goal, just because you like it, and want to do it a little more? You're starting to make me feel guilty (laughing)."

That's all I needed to know about Tom Morey and his compulsion to invent, while definitively answering my earlier question concerning any regrets Tom may have had with his life.

Between two homes, four kids, playful inventions and interest rates at all-time highs, Tom was burning through cash quickly. He decided to renegotiate his deal with Kransco, releasing the worldwide rights for a one-time payment, nullifying his previous royalty agreement.

"...how would you like me out of your hair, cause I got tired of waiting for the check to come, and having to call up the accountant, and the accountant tells me...well we had a problem and this and that...how about the first of next month, and I could see this was going to be the rest of my life talking to this accountant. Then, the next thing they did...I got wind that they had a pair of swim fins that were not a

design I wanted anything to do with, and they were gonna call it Morey swim fins, and so I started raising objections…I started raising a fuss on that."

On March 28, 1983, Kransco filed another trademark application for Morey Swim fins, US Serial #73419180, within the swim fins category.

Tom was able to renegotiate his original deal twice, but it wasn't enough to stop the inevitable.

"I didn't have a job, I didn't have any cash income, so I couldn't borrow any money to do anything…I didn't have credit…loan rates went up to sixteen, seventeen, eighteen percent…and here I am owning two houses with no income, and I'm thinking well, I've gotta make payments, so we had to get out of there, out of that house…and now this credit rating thing becomes another big deal where you just can't borrow from somebody that says, he's a good guy, he'll pay us back, you have to have all this record keeping, and your credit rating goes down if you're late…so there is a devil, and it's all this record keeping, and the money changers that Jesus tried to get rid of back in the day."

Tom's survival instincts kicked in as he sought solutions to alleviate debt, focusing on the computer revolution. IBM and Apple were introducing personal desktop computers, and he recognized the potential of these devices for global transformation, meticulously disassembling one to learn its capabilities.

Influenced by the education tenant of the Bahá'í teachings, he focused on developing a six-disk learning program for kids, named Sound Thinking.

"We also had Sound Thinking (laughing)...and sound thinking (laughing)...I've had quite an adventure. Because I have a background in mathematics and because Marchia's father had given us an Apple IIE computer...I sat down with it with my kid, Sky, and said let's see what we can do with this thing. Sky is all ears, and helpful, and he and I are learning how to use the computer to draw pictures and say things and do all this stuff. So he and I built a series of programs called, Sound Thinking. And it's a disk with a series of programs using the joystick to make music, and you move the joystick forward and backwards and it makes the tones go up and down, and at different speeds...and you can make music with that...and it was great for teaching."

Now all Tom had to do was monetize Sound Thinking into cash, and with another rub on the genie lamp his wish was granted. Or was it?

One day, Tom was driving down the road near his home on the Big Island, when he reconnected with an old friend from his Ventura days, Jim Jalbert.

"Jim Jalbert, one of the two or three most colorful guys I've ever met...this is a guy that, when I started my surf shop in Ventura...I put a sign out on the main road, and he and a couple of buddies were coming from Simi Valley to go surfing...and they saw this sign and tracked me down and found my surf shop, and nosed around, and they

didn't have any money... and they needed a job...I hired a couple of these guys and gave them buckets of tar based silver paint, and they painted my first building...these were classic guys and they were sleeping on the beach, keeping warm piling kelp up around them..."

Tom seemed to be taken by Jalbert's colorful nature, coining him a master salesman. Jim was now married with kids and living from hand-to-mouth, bartering his carpentry skills for living quarters on the Big Island. Their bond was sealed, partly by religious beliefs, as Tom described Jalbert as a savior, someone who was saved and always willing to help those in need.

"...let me go on about good salesman, beyond a good salesman. Jalbert is an experienced land salesman from San Francisco, and from scamming around, I'm not saying scamming as in illegal stuff, but as taking on high risk situations which require a good salesman...he has been selling land through the newspaper and he came up with the world's greatest three word advertisement...cheap...land...and the phone number, those are the three words...and he was a road side fur salesman, and he had his clothesline draped between two trees with furs hanging in between, and his car parked nearby, and women would come in there and look at the furs, and bundle up and take all their clothes off and get in the furs..."

Tom was clear he didn't want me to get the wrong idea about Jim Jalbert, in that he was a moral man and good provider, although I got the impression he closely walked the line between flimflamming and complete honestly when hawking business deals.

"So I developed this malarkey about this thing and my intentions are great, and we're going to sell the thing, and we've got a finished product, and we go off and pitch some of the local people, and we figured out we don't just go out and sell one at a time, we sell a hundred at a time, at a discounted rate...and they owned so many hundred disks, and they don't have to do anything with them, they just own them, and we carry them and we then go ahead and keep selling them, and we pay them their commission."

Jalbert worked his magic with wealthy professionals on the Island, including doctors and dentists, trusting in the credibility of the Tom Morey name to close the sale. It didn't take Jalbert long to close the sale and walk out of prospects with five-thousand-dollar checks, showcasing his master salesmanship, and before long, trusted professionals on the island were spreading the word, encouraging folks to jump on this next big thing. His sales pitch was compelling, advising investors that music departments in schools across the mainland would kill for the Sound Thinking program as a new way to teach music with personal computing. Disappointingly, the genie had to be put back in the bottle.

"What I didn't tell you is, after this thing did not work, and we were wiped out, just like this pandemic is wiping us out (laughing), at that point we got whacked out by the fact that nobody bought five and a quarter inch disks anymore...there were no more floppy disks, and nobody had any machines anymore, and the formats were changing right and left. Now after all this settled down Marchia, bless her

heart…we went back and contacted each of these people and eventually gave them their money back."

Marchia's moral compass outweighed Jalbert's, and she cracked the whip, ensuring his namesake and reputation remained intact. They couldn't pay back investors until both houses were sold, and/or Tom secured a steady stream of income. At the age of fifty, Tom came to the realization it was time to reintroduce himself to corporate America, secure a steady job, and provide for the family.

Tom, Jalbert, and Sol, Tom's oldest son, packed up and headed to Seattle, Washington, home of Boeing, leaving Marchia behind caring for three boys, and selling both homes. Upon arrival, Jalbert headed off to a nearby town to open a used furniture store while Tom and Sol headed to Bainbridge.

"We made the mistake of getting to Seattle on September 20th, the last day of summer…on September 21st, there was no more sunshine…it was just overcast and drizzling, day after day, forever. So we asked people on the street, if you were going to move to the Seattle area, where's the place you would choose, and everybody said Bainbridge Island, so knowing Bainbridge Island was the best place to live, I mean if you don't have anything to lose, you don't head to some place that's second rate, you head to the best place…so I went up there and I called the Bahá'ís on Bainbridge Island, and I got a wonderful gal, Ted and Olga Ruys, and I explained that I was Bahá'í from Hawaii and I was coming up here to make my way, and Olga says, 'well, we have a forty foot trailer off the back property and it's been vacant now and if

you want, you and your boy can live there for a while, and we'll carry your rent...come on up and live here'. So we did that, and she also fronted me a bicycle, since my vehicle had been taken back for lack of payment...I have to get a job...and we're down to very few dollars...so I make an appointment (at Boeing)...and go down to Sears Roebuck with my last credit card, and buy a pinstripe double breasted suit and a briefcase...and I'm taking the bicycle back and forth on the ferry, and after several months of calling and going over there and nagging these people, I get a job as a composite engineer, but they won't call me an engineer, cause I'm not, I'm a mathematician and it's an engineering company, so I get a second rate job over there, where I learned a hell of a lot about composites and had a great time."

Meanwhile, Marchia had fixed up and sold both houses, paid back the Sound Thinking investors, and moved into the trailer with Tom and the kids. Tom wasn't going to let the depressing snow of the Great Northwest damper his creative inspiration.

"...if you're just sitting around, why don't you develop something for the snow...why don't you design a snow boogie. The fact that they (Kransco) told me...it's like telling Stein Eriksen to maybe develop some kind of a new ski, or something."

Dangling the challenge was all it took to jumpstart his genetic compulsion to invent. As a kid, Tom rode a Flexible Flyer, which lacked directional control without toppling over. The focus now was to develop a powerful apparatus for sporting competitions. Together, the boys and Tom began tinkering with aluminum edges designed to cut into the hard packed snow maximizing control as it barreled down the slope. They focused on setting a proper angle to allow banking, constructing the front with a wide single-type ski, the middle platform slightly raised, and the back with camber and two turned-down rudders. Throw in a few sharp bevels, and you've got yourself a snow boogie. After experimenting, they headed out to the competitive ski slopes of Eastern Seattle.

"...I show up at the crowded ski slope, and right away they're telling me I can't get on the chair, you can't take that up there, and if you did you'd need a leash. So I got a dog leash, and I connected it to my ankle and to the board...so I conned my way up there and got some good rides before I wipeout and tear the meniscus in my knee. So, I go to the orthopedic surgeon, and he says, 'you gotta have surgery, we'll take care of it, it takes about fifteen minutes, and it'll cost three thousand bucks, and it'll be good as new.' Well, I'm thinking in my mind, I'm thinking, fuck you, that's sales talk, that pissed me off...you're talking to me, the subconscious being of Tom Morey that has repaired cuts and bruises, I've got scars to prove it. So anyhow, I finally found that glucosamine sulfate was good, and then colloidal minerals were good, and I took these things on a conscientious routine, and it one hundred percent healed..."

The snow boogie idea was abruptly interrupted by a family heartbreak. In 1987, Tom's sister, June, called with sad news. She lived in Tulsa, close to their parents, and stopped by the apartment to periodically caretake. She had just discovered their father had shot their mother, then himself in a lover's pact suicide.

"So my mom and dad were lovers from an early age…he's eighty-nine and she's eighty-three, and she's been falling apart for twenty years. She's had her breast removed, 30 years earlier, and she's full of tumors, and her bones are breaking very easily, and she's in pain all the time, and he's doing pretty good…he's like a rooster…not much fat on him, and he keeps his wits about him, and his coordination up…but mom is so bad, that they have a lover's pack, and finally she gives him the sign that she can't take it anymore, so he shoots her with a .38 pistol four times, shoots her in the head once, and in the body three times. Then he lies down next to her, after scribbling a little note in all lower-case lettering and no punctuation…the note says, specifically, quote 'theres nothing more here for us'…it was a brave, wonderful thing that he did…so there was no tragedy…he did his job."

I was stunned, my mouth dropping open while he described the events. A combination of horror and anguish washed over me, *"Oh my God, man, I'm so sorry to hear that,"* I didn't know what else to say but felt I should console him after he shared such a guarded story. Tom made it clear; I shouldn't be consoling but rather praise his father's actions, given the deep love they had for each other and their commitment to the pact until the very end.

Tom jumped onto a plane to help his sister sort out funeral arrangements and the estate.

"...of the things, I got a late model Pontiac 2 door, and I drove back to Washington in that car...I had a really terrible head cold and flu...and all the boxes and stuff...and two red plastic boxes, each with adhesive backed tape gun labels, one said, Grace, the other one said, Howard...I drove with the responsibility of scattering the ashes, and I thought about a lot of places between Tulsa and Bainbridge Island, and I almost scattered them at the Grand Canyon, and other beautiful sites, but meanwhile I was sick as a dog, driving mostly a lot at night, and I didn't get that job done until I got back to Bainbridge. It's a lovely day and I got out the boxes, and I mix the contents of the two boxes together...in a big stainless steel pan...then we scatter them around some bushes with a plan the next day to drive them out to the end of the country by the old reservation...near the Strait of Juan de Fuca...but I put them back in this plastic bag, and put that whole thing back into the trunk of the car, and when I got ready to go...I looked in the trunk of the car and didn't see it...so I asked Marchia, where's mom and dad, and she says, 'oh, you mean that plastic bag with all those ashes in it, well, it's at the Bainbridge Island dump,' so that's where mom and dad are for the most part."

That story prompted our discussion of end-of-life plans, with me telling Tom I'd like to be paddled out and dumped into the ocean. Tom's position, based on Bahá'í teachings, was to avoid cremation. He felt the ions of human development evolved over an incredibly long period of time and that cremation was a shock to the soul. But by burying the corpse, it allowed the sub-cycles and sub-routines to go back into humanity and life kind.

As part of the estate settlement, Tom and June split the inheritance, leaving Tom one hundred and fifty thousand dollars, which prompted my question, *"did you move back to Southern California?"*

"ABSO-FUCKING-LUTELY." (laughing hysterically)

Tom went into a tirade explaining the astrological nature of living in Bainbridge and the speed of the magnetic field, which is slower in Bainbridge than California. This is based on the longitudinal and latitudinal location of the planet in relation to the sun and moon. Using a pool table and thirteen ball as an example, he was trying to demonstrate the effect by describing the ball rolling against the rail, and how the number disappears and reappears, and how mankind is solidly connected to the universe. Man, I was really lost, so I looked it up and he was correct. The earth moves at different speeds depending on the latitude line, with the fastest movement occurring at the equator and progressively slowing down as you move towards the poles, meaning the earth effectively moves slower at higher latitudes. Bottom line, at latitude 33.4274° N (San Clemente, CA), Tom was moving three to four hundred miles an hour faster than latitude 47.6249° N (Bainbridge Island).

"I'll tell you how it was, we get to the first day of school at Bainbridge Island and you pull up and you drop your kids off…it's overcast, and the girls all have their sweaters on and long sleeve wool things down around their hands to keep them warm…now we get to San Clemente,

and the first day of school, I had taken the kids to the local school, and it's a warm day...gorgeous day in San Clemente in September...and out to the cars come the cheerleaders...for every car that pulls up there's a cheerleader... comes over to the car...opens the door, smiles...these girls are vivacious and they're full of sunlight, they're full of life because that's what's going on down here...major differences in where you live, you know."

One of Tom's favorite astrology books was "Heaven Knows What," by Grant Lewi, originally published in 1935. Morey related to Lewi in several ways, as both deliver accessibility to the masses, Lewi simplifying astrology, and Tom gifting affordable wave riding. The second commonality was the belief that individuals were not realizing their full potential. Tom used Lewi's wise teachings to perform horoscopes for friends and acquaintances, revealing untapped boundaries and worldly goals.

"And one of the paragraphs has to do with...all of a sudden, the impetus gives out, everything's going along fine, I'm very excited, and then a moment later, an hour later, I'm over it...I'm done...the hell with this...that was good...I'm tired of that. So I have that all the time, and then the idea, or the project jumps back into consciousness again, but by then, another one gets involved, and do I really wanna go through all those steps to do that? I think I'm gonna have a cup of coffee or I think I'll go for a walk, or in my case, I'm gonna go surfing."

I totally related to Tom's recurrent motivation and then lack of interest; I call it ADHD, and deal with it frequently. However, when combining a passion project with my

OCD, the obsessive nature powers me through to completion, even though it may be years later. If financial aspirations aren't the driving factor, you tend to chase the fun and discard the commercial element, so when things get difficult, chasing the fun provides an easy excuse to give up and head out to the beach.

"Manufacturing and selling and taking orders and stuff just gets real old real fast...I'm basically an artist...I haven't got any choice, because the art impulsion takes over the commercial part...commerce kind of takes care of itself."

SESSION EIGHT - THE FINAL CALL

Session eight was the last interview charting Tom's life. Our first call was July 6, 2020, and our last September 21, 2020. My color-coded spreadsheet laid out a lifespan of events, and I imagine Tom would have been proud to see how meticulous I organized his life, except he couldn't, at least not very well. Tom had recently undergone several eye surgeries correcting partial blindness. The procedure was funded, in part, by a GoFundMe campaign, spearheaded by Mike Stewart, Morey's daughter, Melinda, and a few friends.

"I don't know how to evaluate it, Mike. It's just…I can't drive a car, I couldn't even think about that, but I can see stuff on the table in front of me, and I can glance at the television, and I can push my button and see that you've called, or not called, it's well lit up on the iPhone."

Not only were his eyes failing, but his mobility was limited to a walker, and although he never would admit it, I suspect his health was declining.

Our discussion returned to happier times, especially his return to California from Bainbridge Island, and life events that played out surrounding the Morey Boogie. In 1994, Morey got wind that Kransco was selling to Mattel. The Wham-O brand included Hula Hoops, Frisbee, Power Wheels, and Morey Boogie, this added one-hundred-and-seventy-five million in annual sales to Mattel, making them the top toy maker in the United States. Tom's name was on the Morey Boogie, and he was furious no one kept him in the loop concerning the sale. The fearless protector of the Morey legacy wrote a letter raising objections, inserting himself directly into the sale.

"...so I had a tentative conversation with the CEO of Mattel...and opened the discussion...and then I found out when was the annual meeting, and I found out it was coming up in just a couple of weeks, so I bought two shares of Mattel from Charles Shwab, and now I attended the shareholders meeting. And that was fun (laughing). So I got the two shares, and I dressed to the nines, and I'm all smiles and niceness, and I get there earlier than anybody else, I'm there greeting everybody, who's this guy (laughing), and I'm sitting in one of the front rows, so I introduce myself to Ned Mansour, Corporate Counsel, and Jill Barad, President/COO, and I'm on a first name basis with Jill. So, there I am... at the meeting coming up in about twenty minutes...so, I tell the boss, CEO (Christopher A. Sinclair),...I say, by the way, if you get stuck on your presentation here, if you'd like me to say a few words, I'd be glad to, I'm sitting right here, so, sure enough, he does that...and he says, 'by the way, on this new move (Kransco purchase), we have the inventor of the boogie board here with us right now, Mr. Tom Morey...Tom, could you say a few words?', so I do that..."

I can tell you from experience that conservative, high profile, public companies don't like potential controversy surrounding their governance, especially a public relations nightmare surrounding the inventor of the Morey Boogie. Tom's audacious episode paid off, netting him a sizeable settlement, and several years of consulting revenue from Mattel, effectively parleying his original sale three times, and why not, both Kransco and Mattel made hundreds of millions of dollars from the sale, and the Morey Boogie was a contributor. Furthermore, out of the entire portfolio of toys, the boogie board was the only one branded to a family legacy, Morey. Tom's veracity to protect his name, coupled with trademark regret, contributed heavily to his lifelong retribution of being a pain in the ass to current and future holders of the trademark, and I for one, applauded his tenacity.

Only three years after Mattel bought Wham-O, Jill Barad, now CEO, divested the Wham-O brand and toy portfolio to a newly formed investment group, Charter House and Seven Hills Partners, led by CEO Michael Cookson. Barad shed the Wham-O division to focus on Barbie and other core brands, which ultimately failed, as she was ousted in 2000 with a reported forty-million-dollar severance. I got the sense Tom liked Cookson's direction for Kransco, as short lived as it was.

"Oh yea, Michael Cookson…he was a very wealthy San Francisco-ite, and he had real heart, and he had real interest…he was a mover

and shaker, but bottom line, little by little, the momentum of the status quo kind of just took the wind out of him, and he made some good moves, and made some nice stuff, and put some good employees in there and he did good, but little by little, he was out of it, out of the whole game...of the whole toy game, the whole toy industry."

In 2006, Cookson's private equity group sold Wham-O to privately held, Hong Kong based, Cornerstone Overseas Investment Limited, a major Chinese toy manufacturer with five factories and worldwide distribution, headed by CEO, Jeff Hsieh. Boogie board brands now included Morey Boogie and BZ Pro Boards.

Once the manufacturing and quality control shifted overseas, Tom's disappointment with the cheapened product negatively affected his Chinese relationship. He felt the business relationship always focused on profit and royalty negotiation, rather than revealing to the world the joy and freedom of surfing.

In 2009, The Aguilar Group purchased Wham-O, headed by Kyle Aguilar and a group of private investors.

In 2016, Joseph Lin, CEO of Stallion Sport, LTD, alongside Intersport Corp. (DBA Wham-O), purchased Wham-O from The Aguilar Group, forming Wham-O Holdings, LTD, based in Hong Kong. Stallion currently holds the Morey trademark, as well as BZ Boards, and Churchill Swim Fins.

A SurferToday article, dated April 9, 2024, entitled, "The Rebirth of Morey Boogie", describes a misunderstanding between the Morey family and Stallion Sport, LTD concerning the proposed launch of the 50th Anniversary Morey Boogie Board. Apparently, while Tom was still living, Wham-O proposed a board coinciding with a series of Tom Morey boogie board events throughout the country, spearheaded by Patti Serrano. Unfortunately, Tom passed before the launch, which prompted the supposed removal of Tom's name and likeness, instead marketing it as a celebration of 50 years of boogie boarding.

I purchased one of these boards at Dick's Sporting Goods. The board is stamped with the first Morey Boogie logo crafted by Craig Libuse with Tepe Paul's long hair flowing, along with the imprint, Morey 50th Anniversary Mach 7 Limited Edition, and it's numbered 160 of 500. If the SurferToday article is correct, this board must have missed the cut before Wham-O changed the design, or another deal was cut with the Morey family. Rumor has it, Mike Stewart and pro bodyboarder Pierre-Louis Costes got involved to assist with the royalty dispute, and the quality of future boards. The Morey Boogie is poised for a resurrection, and Tom would be delighted to know his family and friends are taking over the responsibility of watchdogging the Morey brand, just as he had done the last 50 years.

The earth was spinning faster in San Clemente, but his body slowing, preferably enjoying his prominence as the boogie board man. He would enjoy hanging out at beach events, rapping with the kids about surfing life, and most notably, strumming his ukulele while singing his famed boogie song. I was lucky enough to get a personal rendition, sans the ukulele, during our last session. At eighty-six, I was still impressed with the prodigy musician as he sang the boogie song a cappella.

Corky Carroll had left Tom a message earlier in the day, and Tom had yet to return the call. I mentioned an article that Corky had penned in the Orange County Register, mentioning his connection to the boogie song.

"...it was pretty cute, and I got away with it a lot, and enjoyed it...people to this day ask me to sing the boogie song. (Tom sang for me, a cappella), I just thought about the Pepsi Cola jingle...so anyhow, I've got a friendship with Corky, who's got his own little group of players, and he's written a hundred songs of his own...like, I want to be a surf freak daddy, and drive a surfing van (singing)...so he's got surfing songs like that, with his very cute wife, and two other very cute girls that make up the Corketts, that's Corkey and the Corketts (laughing)...he's clever...and he plays in the clubs and all that."

Tom happened to be hanging out with David Nuuhiwa at a Surfing Heritage Foundation event, where Tom was still pitching a version of his AirSkate idea. There aren't many of these guys left, and I felt lucky, as Tom would say, to be near the fire of this thing, having Tom as my guide.

Our interview was ending, and we discussed how our sessions could transform into some sort of property, either screenplay, book, or even mini-series. I stuck with my initial goal of writing a screenplay, but in retrospect, maybe I should have first authored the book. Like Tom, sometimes I lose interest, only to pick it up again. I'm glad I took a few years off. The time spent boogie boarding cleared my mind refreshing my creative juices, reinforcing my appreciation of our time together.

We had fun throwing around project titles, Tom suggested "The Boogie Man," and I suggested "Shaping Tom Morey," and he agreed.

"Well I'm glad you used that word, because it rings a bell with me, how you shape this surfboard, how you shape this story…every surfboard has a nose, tail, rails…it's got skegs and texture, and all that kind of stuff, but the exact shaping of the wording that you choose and write down and pen (shapes the story)."

I titled the screenplay, "Shaping Tom Morey," but expanded Tom's idea for the book, settling on "Boogie Board Man; Eight Sessions with Thomas Hugh Morey." Tom passed October 14, 2021, and it was a privilege to be one of the last serendipitous characters in Tom's adventurous life, not to mention a ton of fun reminiscing, before giving his soul back into humanity and life kind.

"Great playing with you Mike, we're really doing something here."

As Tom would kiddingly say, *"We're not doing it, we did it."*

EPILOGUE

Tom's colorful storytelling ended, but my journey of realizing the biopic continues.

The challenge of writing the screenplay was daunting. I wrote a few short films, but a feature would take a renewed discipline, and more creative juice, not to mention a totally different format than a book. I turned to The Screenwriter's Bible, by David Trottier (3rd Edition) to brush up on writing guidelines for spec scripts. Spec scripts differ from shooting scripts, in that they focus on telling the story, rather than providing more of a technical format so Hollywood can break it down into a shooting script. When a writer sells a story to Hollywood, it's usually a spec script.

Before physically writing, I needed to figure out a few things.

First, which direction I wanted to go with the story itself. Tom and I discussed how the reality of life can sometimes seem drab and uninteresting, but he appreciated embellishment, as he had done over the last fifty years with the boogie. I wanted the story to stay true to its roots, however some creative license would be required to keep the audience engaged, as long as it didn't stray too far. I decided not to produce a documentary, which is a non-fiction film aimed at accurately presenting historical facts, but rather a biopic, a fictionalized dramatization designed to entertain moviegoers based on true events described in this book. The documentary could possibly be the next project.

Second, how to weave all the complexities of Tom Morey, the character, into the dialogue. Finalizing the screenplay before the book was a novice mistake for many reasons. I went back and reviewed the finished script, and compared that to our session conversations, realizing the dialogue needed further development, especially given how unusual Tom reveals himself.

Third, how to create attention-grabbing conflict within the story without over dramatization, and should I lean more towards a romantic comedy, or romantic drama? The audacious and humorous nature of Tom's personality led me towards romantic comedy, and as for the conflict, several were obvious. Tom's relationships, financial stability, non-conformity, and his obsessive drive to invent.

And finally, working with a cinematographer, the look and feel of the film. I'd lean on my cinematographer to skillfully capture the cultural landscape throughout numerous decades and locations, from the jazz era to present day. I'd especially spotlight the beautiful Hawaiian and Polynesian heritage, incorporating the history of the paipo board, by transitioning from film to animation during Tom's dream sequence while in Christel's closet.

And let's not forget the soundtrack, no limit to the wide range of choices available enhancing the film's mood and energy.

With those elements in mind, I began scriptwriting. The story bounces from present day, back to various points in Tom's life, while hanging out on the beach at a Boogie competition. I won't go into details but rather provide a few nuanced examples of creative license.

Tom's paper hat creation, which was created in the architectural lab at USC and featured in Parade Magazine, was now shaped at El Cholo Mexican restaurant while fiddling with a napkin. I also chose to place a hat on each chair at Tom and Jolly's wedding as a take home gift for guests.

Blending generational culture was especially fun, inserting a group of surfers rapping to Tom at the beach, with him conducting an impromptu rap session back playing his ukelele.

```
          SURFER BOY
          (rap)
His name is Tom Morey he's
the dude of the day/his
playground is the beach and
that's where we play/a
sponger and shaper a really
cool cat/the man who
invented the friggin boogie
mat/so every time we go off
on a wave and eject/we
think of the mad man and
give him our - indelible -
respect.
```

Tom and I would joke about what actor could pull off Tom rapping while playing his ukelele, maybe Steve Martin, Dick Van Dyke, William H. Macy, Jon Voight, or even Adam Sandler. It would definitely be fun working with a casting director selecting actors.

Comically, I inserted a foreshadow naming the SNAKE machine. I thought it would be fun combining Tom's disdain for English professors, with his love of acronyms.

PROFESSOR
Mr. Morey

Tom snaps head up off desk.

PROFESSOR
Please wipe that drool off
the desk.

Tom grabs the tail of his shirt and
cleans desk.

PROFESSOR
While I am enthralled with
your extraordinary musical
talent...I mean performing
alongside luminaries such
as Stu Williamson, Conti
Candoli, Bud Shank and even
the great Dizzy Gillespie...I
still suspect you'll always
be a SNAKE.

The class murmurs.

PROFESSOR
Relax people. It's an
acronym. Surfers Not
Applying Knowledge
Effectively.

I took a cue from Tom's audaciousness and created a scene when Tom returns home from Kaua'i after purchasing the four-acre home to find Jolly in bed with John Bubinski. Tom and Jolly end up eating chocolate ice cream (the removal of all difficulties) in the kitchen while calmly discussing their eventual move to Hawaii. I didn't think this was a huge stretch, since Tom, Jolly, and John eventually lived together at Kanashiro's hippy shack. I jokingly quote Tom saying, *"I like Bubi."*

On the other end of the spectrum, Tom loved to shape boards, gently flowing his hands along the contours of the deck, searching for imperfections. Why not apply this soft touch with Marchia?

INT. APARTMENT - DAY

TOM AND MARCHIA IN BED

            Roommate (OS)
   I'm off to work. Don't be
   late, you're prepping
   lunch.

            MARCHIA
   Ok.

                         TOM
        I couldn't have shaped a
        better body if I had done
        it myself. The perfect nose
        angle, the stringer running
        straight down the center,
        the smooth deck and
        slightly contoured rails
        running down to a perfect
        tail. Oops, I think I found
        a tiny ding, I may have to
        fill it.

The sensitivity of this scene is up to the actors and intimacy coordinator, but I couldn't resist adding a hint of sensual bravado to Tom's character, especially knowing his tenderness for Marchia.

One of my personal favorites is the scene where Tom meets Dewey Weber. At the end of our final session, I asked Tom to describe everyone mentioned throughout his story. The background and intimate knowledge of each character would be helpful for actors and character development. Tom liked to call Dewey Weber, Dew-Dew-Wee-Wee. He never said why, but I couldn't resist blending his board shaping obsessiveness with some Morey humor. The following is how he described Dewey, followed by the scene.

"Dew — Dew — Wee - Wee. Dewey Weber was flamboyant...at a very young age he was the boy in the shoe in the Buster Brown commercial...Hi, my name's Buster Brown, I live in a shoe, here's my dog Tige, he lives there too. It was a famous shoe ad for Buster Brown shoes. Then...he became the California State yo-yo champion. In high school, he was a star wrestling champion. He was in a few surf movies, and I befriended him one day in the restroom, I was peeing, and he was peeing, and I said, hey Dewey, you did great in that movie, man, you were terrific. And we became friends, shortly thereafter I rode on his surf team."

INT. HIGH SCHOOL AUDITORIUM - NIGHT

A white poster hangs with black and white surfer photo and bright red print.

"Bud Browne Presents
LOCKED IN!
color surf film
Sponsored by Santa Barbara Surf Club
SANTA BARBARA
HI SCHOOL AUD.
WEDNESDAY - SEPT 9TH
8:15 p.m.
Admission $1.50 - Tickets at Door"

The projectionist feeds film into projector as movie screen sets up.

Students admire celebrity surfers.
The film begins. The seats fill.

Tom enters high school and wanders
hall for bathroom. He enters and
meanders to urinal, DEWEY WEBER on
left, student on right.

                STUDENT
        Nice meeting you Dewey.

                DEWEY
        Enjoy the movie kid.

                DEWEY
                (to Tom)
        Are you checking out my we-
        we?

Tom peaks and shrugs.

                TOM
        Feel that spray on your
        legs? Just like dropping
        into six foot waves with a
        standing wind. I'm putting
        an orbicular shaped urinal
        on my fabrication list.

                    DEWEY
You've got to aim high and
drop into the corner. Now I
know why they call you the
mad scientist.

                    TOM
Let's call it an inventive
fetish.

                    DEWEY
I like your style man,
mellow.

Tom wiggles and aims for perfect
stream angle.
                    DEWEY
You still with Con?

Dewey zips up, flushes, and washes
hands.

                    TOM
    Team less.

Tom holds the angle of his stream.

                    TOM
    There it is.

>   DEWEY
> We've got a spot if you're
> interested.

>   TOM
> I'm getting sick of riding
> archaic boards made by guys
> in wood shop, man. I'm
> looking for true observers
> of hydrodynamics.

>   DEWEY
> My boards are bitchin fast
> and cut through water like
> butter. Stop by the shop
> and we'll work it out.

>   TOM
> Sounds great, DEW-DEW-WEE-
> WEE.

Dewey exits.

Tom zips up, rinses towel and wipes
off hands and legs. He opens
auditorium doors and gets a glimpse
of Dewey's surfing footage on screen.
Tom scans the audience, Hobie and
Sharon sitting together.

BACK TO PRESENT

That's only a sampling of the creative license producing the biopic into an entertaining story. After brushing off the Morey project and reviewing the interview sessions, it's obvious the screenplay requires polishing, maybe even a total rewrite, which isn't uncommon when a spec script is sold to Hollywood. I sent the treatment to several production companies, and most recently, have submitted the story to scriptwriting competitions. I'd rather write than sell, and rejection often leads to lack of interest, like Tom, I prefer to go surfing.

I'm saddened Tom departed prior to finishing the book. He would have loved the final product, controlling the narrative, on his terms, but I'm positive he's still sticking his nose between every word, helping to shape the script into a cinematic masterpiece.

I for one, can't wait to enjoy the show!

****

I'm always looking to improve my storytelling and would love to hear your HONEST feedback. I read all reviews and encourage you to leave one on Amazon, or my Goodreads Author page.

Enjoy the Stoke!

BOOGIE BOARD MAN

Interview Preparation Material and Credit

Mike Del Ninno
Eight Session Audio Interview with Tom Morey
Screenplay Biopic, "Shaping Tom Morey"
youtube.com/@nmdelninno, Bodyboarding Playlist
****

Surfline.com
Dashel Pierson, "Surf Community Rallies to Support Tom Morey," Nov 14th, 2017
Simon Ramsey, "Bodyboarders vs Surfers, a Retrospective," Feb 20th, 2019
****

Orange County Register
Corky Carroll, "Anecdotes shed light on Boogie Board icon," August 5, 2011
Laylan Connelly, "Special Guest at Beach – Tom Morey," August 13, 2019
****

SurferToday.com
Seamus McGoldrick, "A Short Biography of Tom Morey"
Luís Madureira Pinto, "The outstanding bodyboarding life of Patti Serrano"
Luís Madureira Pinto, "The Morey Boogie factory in Carlsbad"
Luís Madureira Pinto, "Craig Libuse: the story of Morey Boogie's art director"
"The bodyboard celebrates its 50th anniversary", July 7, 2021
Luís Madureira Pinto, "The musical side of Tom Morey"
"The 1985 mini-documentary on the Morey Boogie board", May 14, 2018
Luís Madureira Pinto, "What is a paipo?"
Luís Madureira Pinto, "Morey Boogie Land: Tom Morey's 1980s wave pool vision"
"Tom Morey's eyesight has improved by 20 percent", January 21, 2019
****

BeachGrit.com
Derek Rielly, "(Ancient) Blood Feud: Boogie Riders vs Stand-ups!"
****

SurfBoardLine.com
Posted by Mark, "Morey-Pope," Apr 7th, 2010
****

BOOGIE BOARD MAN

SFGATE.COM

Pia Sarkar, Chronicle Staff Writer, "John Bowes -- businessman and art collector," Oct 28, 2005
Carolyne Zinko, Chronicle Staff Writer, "John Rosekrans, toy executive, Spreckels heir," Oct 30, 2001
****

SanDiegoReader.com
Gordon Smith, Author, "Boogie boards got their start in Carlsbad," Publish Date Aug. 24, 1978
****

Today.USC.edu
Eric Lindberg, "Tom Morey, 86, surfing legend and Boogie board inventor", October 18, 2021
****

Vault.si.com (Sports Illustrated Vault)
Franz Lidz, "The Ocean Speaks to You," Original Publish May 10, 1982
****

MyPaipoBoards.org
Bob Green, "A Paipo Interview with Vinny Bryan", January 26, 2010
****

Pasadena Independent Star News
Jolly Givens / Tom Morey Wedding Announcement, Page 35, Dec 21, 1958
****

LastWave.com
Legends: MOREY-POPE SURFBOARDS & DALE VELZY
****

www.eos.surf/encyclopedia/morey-tom
hobiesurfshop.com/
gordonandsmith.com/pages/history
matthewmarks.com/artists/ken-price
astrologysoftware.com/pro/win_writer/heaven_knows.html
Baháí.org
****